40+ 'DRAMA' STRATEGIES TO DEEPEN WHOLE CLASS LEARNING

'Drama' strategies are great teaching tools that can easily become part of every teacher's toolbox. *40+ 'Drama' Strategies to Deepen Whole Class Learning* is a practical handbook for teachers of any subject. It can help teachers to confidently incorporate 'drama' strategies within their lessons. This book provides step-by-step instructions on setting up and effectively using strategies to make lessons more interactive, inclusive, engaging, enjoyable, and memorable, whilst acknowledging the benefits of each and demonstrating how they may be applied within different subjects.

Divided into two distinct parts, this essential guide unpacks topics including the following.

- An introduction to using 'drama' strategies to support teaching and learning.
- Using the strategies within the classroom as 'thought and talk' frames.
- Supporting and improving writing through application of the strategies.
- Creating, exploring, and embodying images through the strategies.
- A guide to each of the 40+ strategies.

Applicable to both primary and secondary teaching, across all subjects in the curriculum, this book is an essential resource for any teacher looking to engage their pupils through incorporating 'drama' teaching and learning strategies within their lessons.

Patrice Baldwin is an internationally acclaimed 'Drama for Learning' specialist. She is Chair of the Council for Subject Associations (UK) and a Higher Level Action Learning Facilitator. She has worked as a headteacher, School Improvement and Arts Adviser, school inspector, national curriculum consultant, Chair of National Drama (2004-2015) and President of the International Drama/Theatre and Education Association (2010-2013), and as a BBC Education consultant and scriptwriter.

'This is a book that turns the learning ambition into reality in the classroom. The teacher is provided with clearly explained strategies that will engage children in their learning and take thinking and understanding to new levels. Every staffroom needs a copy.'

Professor Mick Waters

'I have worked with Patrice Baldwin, I have taken part in her workshops and I've heard her share her strategies and insights on how it's possible to engage every child in every classroom. Every encounter with Patrice has been brilliant, energising and thought-provoking. I am so glad she has written this book. It's an invitation to take the children in our classrooms to places of deep learning and it's an absolute boon to the sector.'

Mary Myatt, education writer and speaker, curator *Myatt & Co.*

40+ 'DRAMA' STRATEGIES TO DEEPEN WHOLE CLASS LEARNING

A Toolbox for ALL Teachers

Patrice Baldwin

With all good wishes,

Patrice Baldwin

June 2024

Routledge
Taylor & Francis Group

LONDON AND NEW YORK

Designed cover image: © Getty Images

First published 2024
by Routledge
4 Park Square, Milton Park, Abingdon, Oxon OX14 4RN

and by Routledge
605 Third Avenue, New York, NY 10158

Routledge is an imprint of the Taylor & Francis Group, an informa business

© 2024 Patrice Baldwin

The right of Patrice Baldwin to be identified as author of this work has been asserted in accordance with sections 77 and 78 of the Copyright, Designs and Patents Act 1988.

All rights reserved. No part of this book may be reprinted or reproduced or utilised in any form or by any electronic, mechanical, or other means, now known or hereafter invented, including photocopying and recording, or in any information storage or retrieval system, without permission in writing from the publishers.

Trademark notice: Product or corporate names may be trademarks or registered trademarks, and are used only for identification and explanation without intent to infringe.

British Library Cataloguing-in-Publication Data
A catalogue record for this book is available from the British Library

Library of Congress Cataloging-in-Publication Data
Names: Baldwin, Patrice, author.
Title: 40+ 'drama' strategies to deepen whole class learning : a toolbox for all teachers / Patrice Baldwin.
Other titles: Forty plus 'drama' strategies to deepen whole class learning
Description: London ; New York : Routledge, 2024. | Includes bibliographical references and index.
Identifiers: LCCN 2023049445 (print) | LCCN 2023049446 (ebook) | ISBN 9781032380179 (hardback) | ISBN 9781032380186 (paperback) | ISBN 9781003343080 (ebook)
Subjects: LCSH: Drama in education.
Classification: LCC PN3171 .B247 2024 (print) | LCC PN3171 (ebook) | DDC 371.39/9–dc23/eng/20230104
LC record available at https://lccn.loc.gov/2023049445
LC ebook record available at https://lccn.loc.gov/2023049446

ISBN: 978-1-032-38017-9 (hbk)
ISBN: 978-1-032-38018-6 (pbk)
ISBN: 978-1-003-34308-0 (ebk)

DOI: 10.4324/9781003343080

Typeset in Interstate
by Apex CoVantage, LLC

CONTENTS

Introduction   vi

PART 1

1   Using the strategies to support teaching and learning   3

2   Using the strategies as 'thought and talk' frames   14

3   Using the strategies to support and improve writing   23

4   Using the strategies to make and explore images   29

PART 2

5   The 'Drama' strategies   37

Bibliography   103
Index   105

INTRODUCTION

There are books about active learning and there are books about drama strategies, but this book is different. It lifts 'drama' strategies away from drama and presents them more generally as teaching and learning strategies which can be used by any class teacher for the teaching of any subject. Forget the word 'drama' and look at the 40+ strategies in this book as pedagogical tools that can be used by class teachers and subject teachers to the benefit of both teachers and learners.

There are dozens of highly effective interactive teaching and learning strategies, many of which are used in drama lessons and are referred to as drama strategies. It is time for these strategies to become more generally known and used as 'teaching and learning' strategies for any lesson. The strategies in this book can be part of any teacher's toolbox. They can be used to get pupils thinking and talking together about any subject matter and communicating their knowledge and understanding of it in a range of ways. If teachers decide to choose a strategy that requires the pupils to briefly 'perform' in some way, the focus can stay on the subject matter and what the pupils are revealing and communicating about their knowledge and understanding of it.

The strategies in this book help make learning and teaching enjoyable, social, inclusive, interactive, collaborative, engaging and memorable. Most teachers probably know one or two 'drama' strategies but may tend to use them repeatedly, in the same way. This book offers some variations for commonly used strategies and introduces plenty of different strategies, too. Brief examples are given as to how various strategies can be used when teaching Literacy and English, Languages, or the Arts and Humanities.

This book has two parts. Part 1 consists of four chapters that each look at the strategies, through different lenses. This is intended to make it easier for teachers to select strategies which will best meet the needs of their pupils and the learning intentions of the lesson. Part 2 presents the 40+ strategies in turn, with clear instructions and suggestions as to why, how, and when teachers might use each of the strategies and how some might easily follow on from each other.

Chapter 1 sets out the main configurations and groupings that most strategies use and briefly explains how different strategies might share the same or similar configurations, yet have different protocols which intentionally might shift the focus of pupils and vary their levels of freedom to move, speak, make sounds, and interact with each other in various ways.

Chapter 2 explains how strategies can be selected and set up by teachers in various ways to stimulate, require, and enable pupils to use different types of thinking and inter-thinking, and to give them practise at using different types of talk in increasingly challenging ways. Types of talk are briefly outlined and cross-referenced to some strategies which may be particularly useful for practising various types of talk. Ways in which strategies can be sequenced or combined to deepen thinking and sustain pupils' talk are also highlighted.

Chapter 3 explains how strategies can be selected, set up, and sometimes sequenced to get pupils to talk in certain ways as preparation for writing in various styles and forms. Strategies are highlighted that will help pupils to explore and create settings, characters, and plots. Also, the way strategies can be set up to generate different types of talk before asking pupils to embark on different types of writing are explained, and the possible roles of the teacher during the strategies and the various stages of the writing process are also considered.

Chapter 4 focuses on the way that strategies can be used to explore and understand existing images and be used to get pupils creating their own images. Subject-specific examples are offered, highlighting how certain strategies might be used with images during English, History, Geography and Personal Social Health Economic (PSHE) and Relationships Education, as well as Art and Design lessons. The ways in which various strategies can be used to give pupils opportunities to study, visualise, form, hold, extend, melt, deconstruct, juxtapose, and sequence images are briefly explained and exemplified.

Chapter 5 is a rich toolbox of 40+ strategies, presented and explained in turn. What the strategy offers learning and teaching is outlined first, then step-by-step instructions are given for teachers to follow when they are setting up the strategy with their classes. Brief subject-specific examples are provided as to when and how the strategy might be used, and there are often 'Teachers Tips' added, too. Strategy variations and possible follow-on strategies are also highlighted. Ways of recording what has been thought and said during some of the strategies are suggested, where appropriate.

This book is first and foremost a resource for class teachers of any subject. It is not a recipe book to be slavishly followed. It is hoped that teachers will try some of the 40+ strategies in various lessons and feel free to adapt them as necessary to match their own teaching needs and the learning needs of the pupils they teach. Hopefully, teachers of any subject who read this book will soon find themselves thinking about when and how they might start using some of these strategies in their lessons.

PART 1

1 Using the strategies to support teaching and learning

'Drama' strategies can be used as teaching and learning tools. Any teacher can learn how to set up the strategies and use them to support deep learning in any curriculum subject. The strategies can be simplified or made more challenging by teachers and can be adapted for pupils of any age. Forget the word 'drama' and substitute instead 'active' or 'interactive' strategies that get pupils out of their seats, using their bodies and senses, and thinking and talking in various ways.

Most teachers are familiar with just one or two 'drama' strategies, usually 'Hot-seating' (Section 5.17) and 'Freeze-frame' (Section 5.11), yet there are dozens of strategies that can be used effectively in classrooms – with whole classes. The more strategies that any teacher knows and uses, the more skilled they will become at selecting and applying them purposefully in various subject lessons and across the curriculum.

In drama lessons, pupils are often working 'in role' but many of the strategies do not require the pupils (or teachers) to be 'working in role'. Some of the strategies do include an element of 'performance' but whenever this is the case, the prime focus can be intentionally pedagogical rather than theatrical.

> There is no historically or culturally fixable limit to what is or is not 'performance' . . . The underlying notion is that any action that is framed, enacted, presented, highlighted, or displayed is a performance.
>
> Richard Schechner (2006, page 2)

Groupings and configurations

Drama strategies employ a wide range of groupings and configurations. Some require the class to stand or sit in one or more class circles. Others require them to get into one or more straight lines. Some strategies require pupils to work individually, whereas others give them opportunities to work in pairs, small groups, or as a whole class. Some strategies have fixed groups, whereas others require pupils to move around (at will, or when directed to do so) and interact in new pairs and groups. Some strategies get pupils working 'face to face', whereas others require them to work 'back to back' or 'blind', with no eye contact.

The class circle

For centuries, 'the circle' has been used by communities for discussing, problem-solving, decision-making, and presenting. The use of circles for democratic, whole-class discussion is well established and many teachers are probably familiar with the use of 'Circle Time' in schools. 'Circle Time' is rooted in the work of the social scientist Jacob Moreno (1946), who founded psychodrama and sociodrama. 'Circle Time' became popular in UK schools during the 1990s and became mainly used in the teaching of personal, social, health, and emotional education (Mosley, 1996; Mosley and Tew, 1999).

Several drama strategies start with the class sitting or standing in a class circle (usually facing inwards). The teacher often joins their pupils and becomes part of the class circle, too.

Working in circles, enables the following.

- Eye contact.
- Verbal and non-verbal communication.
- Social and inter-personal connection.
- A sense of equal status and equal responsibility.
- Inclusion and a sense of belonging to a community.
- A central focal point that can be used.

Some drama strategies require everyone to stay in their fixed positions in the circle, whereas some strategies invite or require pupils to move and change positions at times, e.g. during 'Passing Thoughts' (Section 5.24), if pupils choose to cross the circle and speak, then they end up standing on the opposite side of the circle (Figure 1.1).

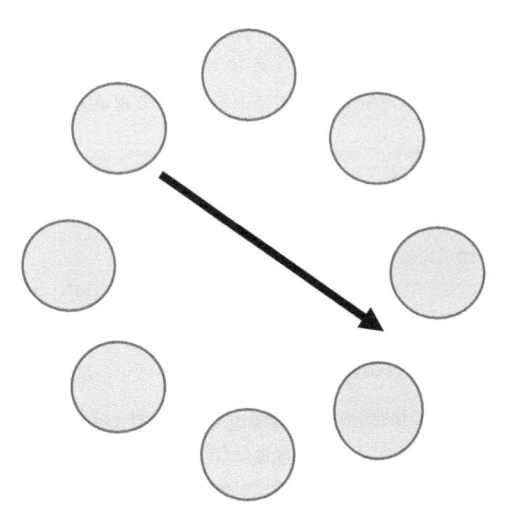

Figure 1.1 'Passing Thoughts' (crossing the circle)

During a 'Whoosh!' (Section 5.10), the pupils in turn leave their positions at the edge of the circle, step forward and mime for a while, and then return to their original place in the circle (Figure 1.2).

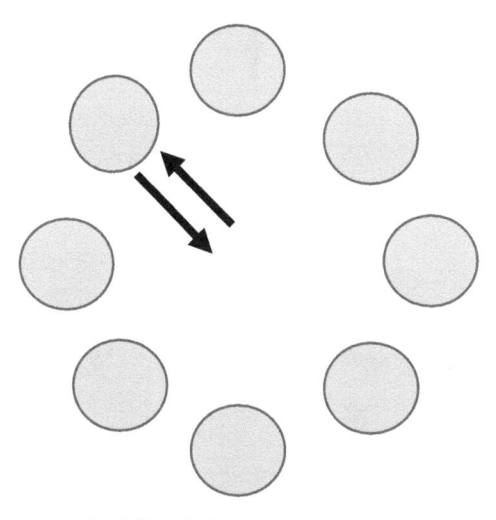

Using the strategies to support teaching and learning 5

Figure 1.2 'Whoosh!' (in and out of the circle)

A class circle enables pupils to easily get themselves into pairs by simply turning to face the person standing next to them (Figure 1.3). From time to time, the teacher can signal for one of the pair to move along the circle and face their next partner, e.g. all the pupils facing clockwise might be asked to 'Move on', whilst all the pupils facing anti-clockwise will be asked to stay still and wait for their new partner to arrive.

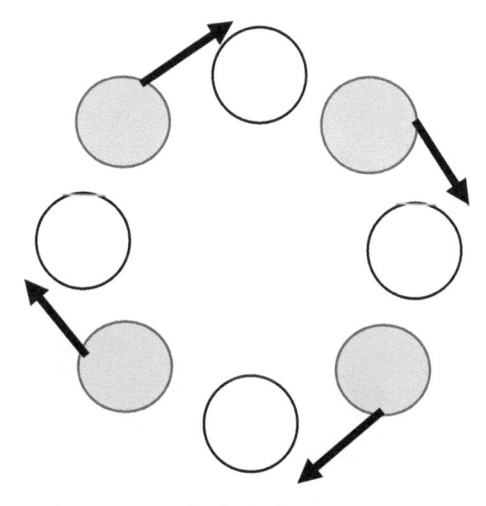

Figure 1.3 Talking Partners (one moves clockwise)

In a class circle, pupils can be asked to face outwards and close their eyes (Figure 1.4). Having eyes closed gives pupils a sense of privacy, removes visual distractions, and can help pupils to focus. Everyone can then be asked to open their eyes, face inwards again, and maybe share their thinking.

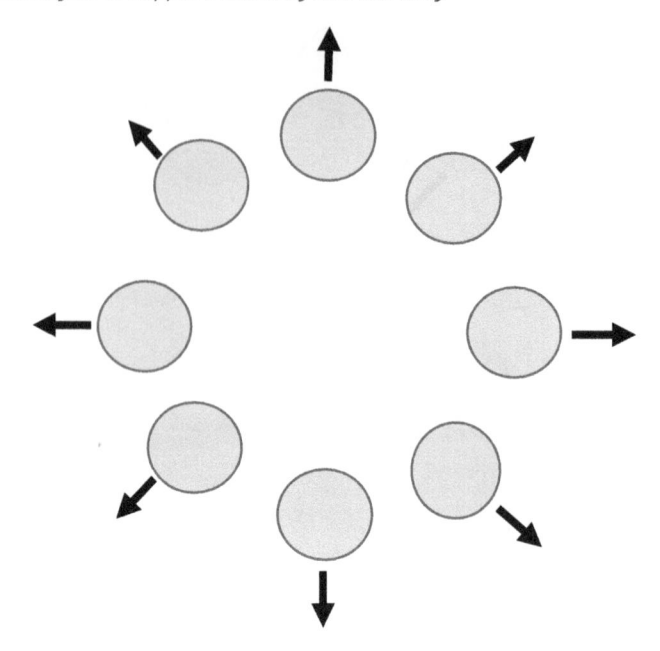

6   *Using the strategies to support teaching and learning*

Figure 1.4 Facing outwards and 'blind'

The space inside a circle provides a focal point which can be used for presentations or performances 'in the round' (Figure 1.5). Individuals or groups can, in turn, be invited to enter the space to present their ideas or perform to their peers.

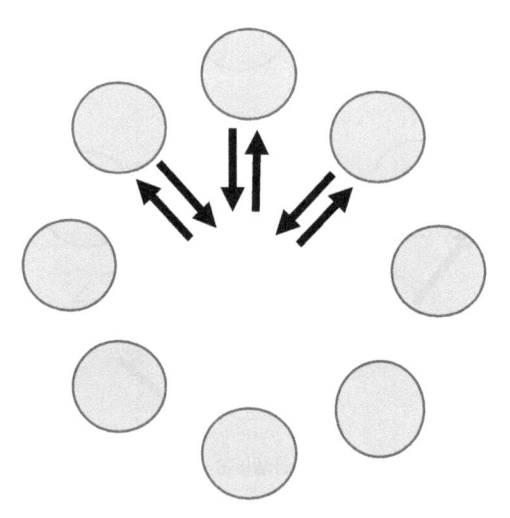

Figure 1.5 Performing 'in the round'

A 'speaking object' – such as a feather, shell, or stick – can be ritualistically passed around a class circle. Whoever is holding the object has the opportunity to speak without interruption, before passing the object on to the next person in the circle. If someone does not want to speak, they take the object and just pass it on silently to the next person (Figure 1.6).

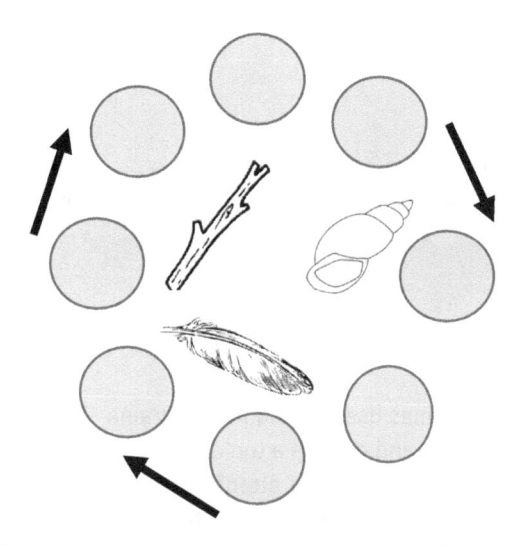

Figure 1.6 Pass 'it' on

Pupils standing in a circle can be asked to each enter the space in turn, and position themselves meaningfully in relation to something of significance that has been placed in the centre. In drama, this is referred to as 'Proxemics' (Section 5.25), and pupils might be asked (for example) to position themselves in relation to a character who is standing in the centre. However, in other subject lessons, they could be asked to position themselves in relation to a centrally placed word, statement, opinion, or idea, e.g. 'Plastic containers should be banned'. Each pupil justifies and explains their relative positioning.

Concentric circles

A class can be asked to form two circles, with one circle inside the other. The person standing opposite them (in the other circle) can become their immediate partner. The pupils can then interact in pairs until the teacher signals for them to stop and change partners. Then the pupils in just one of the circles all move along one place, so that everyone ends up facing their next partner (Figure 1.7).

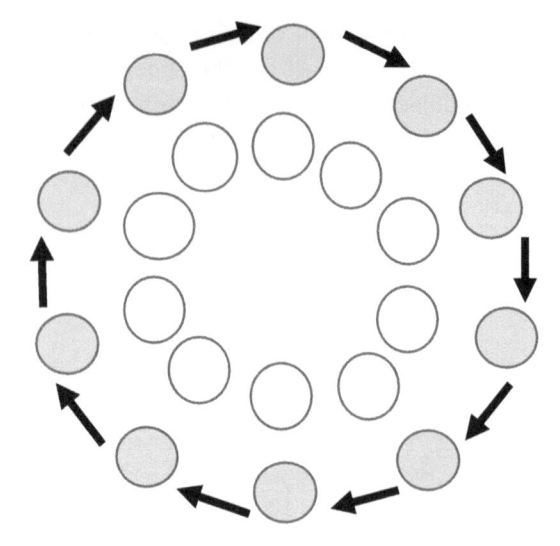

8 *Using the strategies to support teaching and learning*

Figure 1.7 Changing partners (one circle moves)

Concentric circles are sometimes used during psychodrama. Those seated in the inner circle all face forward as a group and discuss a topic or issue for a while. Those seated in the outer circle sit behind them, just listening attentively. When those within the inner circle have finished their discussion, then those in the outer circle are given time to openly question them, respond to what they have heard, and give feedback to those in the inner circle (Figure 1.8).

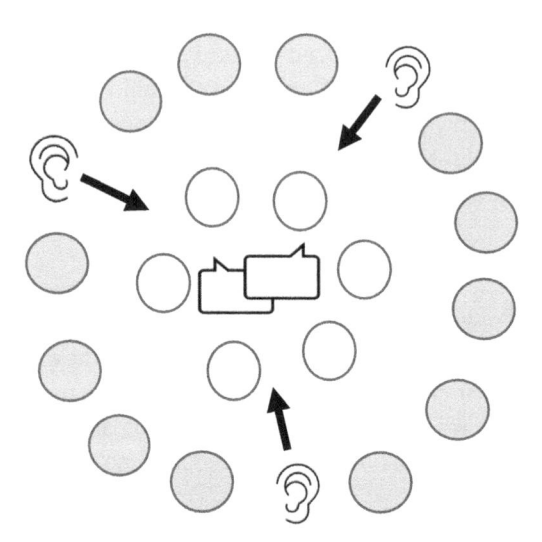

Figure 1.8 Talkers and listeners (inner and outer circles)

Group circles

Whole classes can split into smaller group circles for focused discussions (and for devising presentations and short performances). The class can then either reform a class circle (or semi-circle) to share their group outcomes in turn, or each group can stay where they are and present or perform in a 'Performance Carousel' (Section 5.16) (Figure 1.9).

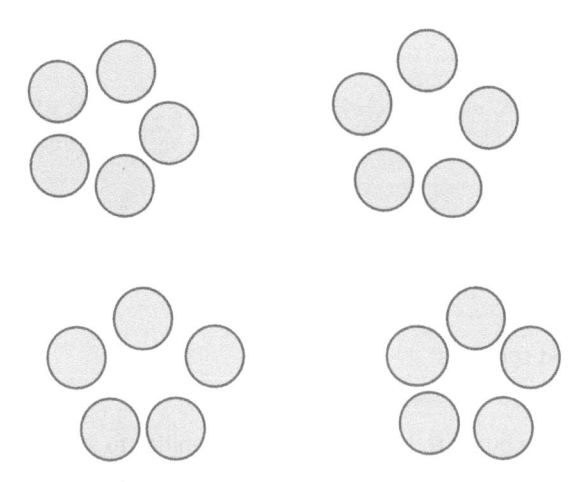

Figure 1.9 Clusters and carousels

One line

The teacher indicates where a long imaginary line has been drawn on the floor. The opposite ends of the line will represent opposing viewpoints or opinions about a specific issue, e.g. each pupil in turn joins the line at the point that fits with where they stand on the given issue (see 'Spectrum of Difference/Spectrogram', Section 5.26) (Figure 1.10).

Figure 1.10 Standpoints

Two lines

For a 'Conscience Alley' (Section 5.19), a 'Decision Alley' (Section 5.20), a 'Thought Tunnel' (Section 5.21), or a 'Corridor of Voices' (Section 5.22), the pupils get into two long lines and face each other. During a drama lesson, a character usually walks between the two lines. Those standing in opposite lines may speak the character's conflicting thoughts aloud, as he/she passes each person in turn (see 'Conscience Alley', Section 5.19) (Figure 1.11). This configuration helps ensure that all pupils get an opportunity to speak to (or about) the character passing by each of them.

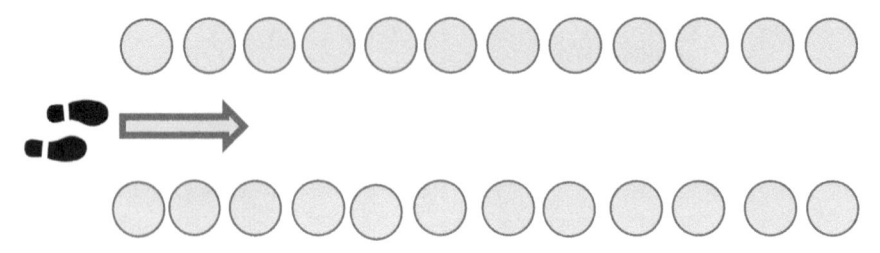

Figure 1.11 Tunnels and corridors

If the teacher wants the pupils to have several opportunities to speak, they can move back and forth between the lines several times. Alternatively, the two lines can become continuous, if the pairs of pupils at the head of each line break away and rejoin their lines at the opposite end once the character has passed by (Figure 1.12).

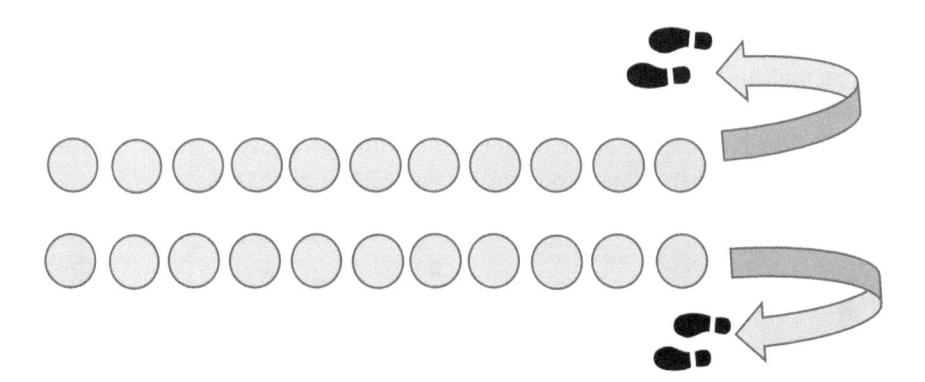

Figure 1.12 Continuous lines

When the class is split into two lines and the pupils are facing each other, the pupils can be asked to talk with the person opposite them and/or then to those standing on either side of them. All pupils can have a new partner if the teacher asks those standing in just one of the lines to move along one place (Figure 1.13). The pupil at the front of the moving line leaves it and rejoins the line at the other end.

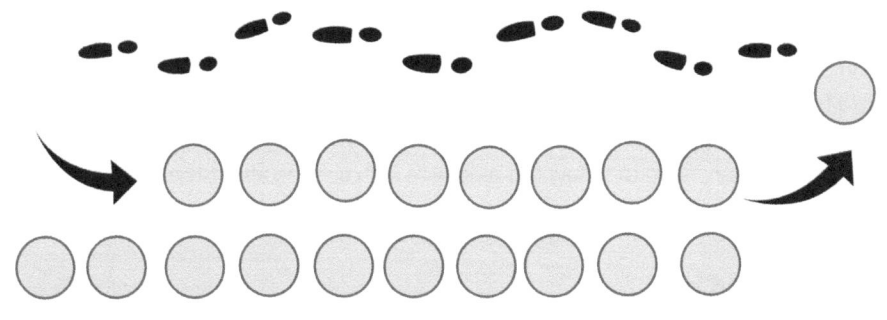

Figure 1.13 One line moves

'Staging' columns

Anything that has already been written down in columns can be staged and shared out loud, i.e. performed. Conversely, what will subsequently be written in columns can be voiced on stage first (with the stage space sectioned into columns) (Figure 1.14). Each pupil in turn enters and stands in one of the columns and speaks to an imaginary audience, voicing aloud something that belongs in that column.

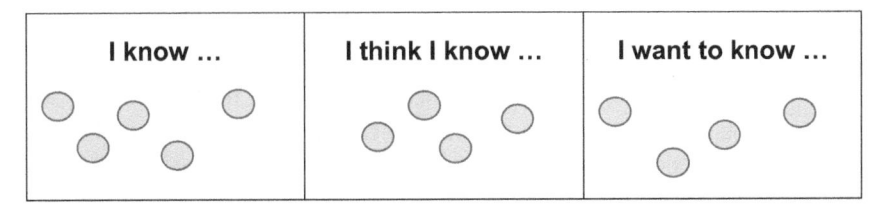

Figure 1.14 Staging columns

If the pupils are reading Shakespeare's *Macbeth* (for example), they can each enter a column and say what they know, think they know and/or want to know at various points during the play, e.g. 'I know Macbeth has just stabbed Duncan' or 'I think I know that no-one saw the murder happen' and 'I want to know what Lady Macbeth will do with the bloody dagger'.

Staging columns can be used in any curriculum subject. During a History lesson, for example, when the pupils are learning about an historical character or event, they can physically position themselves in columns and say what they know about the event, what they think they know about it (and might need to verify), and what they want to know about it (and can then go and find out).

Freedom and constraint

The 'drama' strategies each have different protocols. Some allow freedom of speech and movement, e.g. 'Improvisation' (Section 5.1), whereas others are more restrictive, e.g. mime is silent and 'Freeze-frame' (Section 5.11) are static. 'Rumours' (Section 5.7) invites pupils to all move around the room and chat with each other. Some strategies require pupils to await their turn before being allowed to talk or move, e.g. 'Conscience Alley' (Section 5.19) and 'Whoosh!' (Section 5.10). Some strategies allow each pupil to decide for themselves, when and whether to take a turn at talking and/or moving, e.g. 'Passing Thoughts' (Section 5.24). During a 'Voice Collage' (Section 5.32) or 'Sound Collage' (Section 5.34), pupils judge when to speak and/or make sounds, as they need to follow the teacher's instructions about the overall volume and frequency of their collaborative contributions.

Teachers, in and out

When teachers join in strategies alongside their pupils, it signals a temporary and imaginary shift, in the usual teacher-pupil relationship status. This can be liberating and surprisingly productive, for both the pupils and the teacher. Teachers can choose whether to join in alongside their pupils, during some strategies, e.g. 'Collective Role' (Section 5.30). However, the teacher's participation is necessary for some strategies, e.g. 'Teacher-in-Role' (Section 5.2). During a 'Conscience Alley' (Section 5.19), the teacher is usually the person walking between the two lines of pupils, and during 'Eavesdropping' (Section 5.5), it is usually the teacher who moves around the room, listening in to various conversations, and ensuring they are being heard by everyone.

When teachers do join in the strategies, they should have a purpose in mind. For example, a teacher might join in 'Rumours' (Section 5.7) to feed in some authentic information and/or emphasise certain rumours. Teachers can choose to be the person being questioned during the 'hot-seating' (Section 5.17) to impart significant information to the class and stimulate further questioning. If a pupil is in the 'hot-seat', then the teacher might decide to become one of the questioners, perhaps to model good questioning and/or to focus the pupils' attention in certain directions.

Social and inclusive

Some strategies require pupils to work individually, but they usually will be working collaboratively – in pairs, or groups of various sizes, or as a whole class. Most pupils enjoy the social, interactive, and inclusive nature of strategies, and they are particularly effective when everyone is contributing at some point.

The strategies are inclusive and teachers should ideally avoid excluding any pupils and letting them just sit out and watch, (particularly for behaviour reasons). It is advisable to let pupils signal 'pass' if/when it comes to their turn if they do not feel able or willing to contribute at that moment. Neither the teacher or other pupils should comment if any pupil silently signals, 'pass'. Similar protocols about 'passing' apply during 'Circle Time' and appear in whole class drama contracts (Baldwin, 2008, page 23).

Voice and body

Drama strategies often require pupils to use speech, sounds, gestures, and/or movements to communicate meaning. Pupils may be asked to use their bodies and/or their voices individually, sequentially, randomly, or in unison.

Linking learning to speech, sound, movement, and gesture makes the learning more memorable and retrievable in a range of ways. The use of mime, voice, and 'embodied cognition' is at the forefront of the 'Talk for Writing' approach which originated in Italy, was introduced through the National Strategies in England, and has since been significantly developed and popularised by Pie Corbett (Corbett and Strong, 2011). The class repeatedly tells and retells the same story in unison, joining in with their teacher and making specific gestures whenever they speak certain words and phrases during the storytelling. The pupils are literally 'remembering' a given story together, before becoming innovative with it later.

Drama strategies that involve miming a story include 'Active Storytelling' (Section 5.9) and 'Whoosh!' (Section 5.10). During 'Active Storytelling', the teacher is usually telling and miming the story, with the pupils initially imitating and miming whatever the teacher is saying and doing. A 'Whoosh!' is slightly more innovative at the outset, as it gives pupils opportunities to create their own mime spontaneously, improvising actions 'in the moment', rather than just copying the teacher's.

Stillness and movement

Some drama strategies require pupils to stay very still, whereas others require them to move for some or all of the time, and occasionally in slow motion. Some strategies require movement and stillness at different times, e.g. a 'Freeze-frame' (Section 5.11) is arrived at by freezing movement, and a 'Performance Carousel' (Section 5.16) only allows one group at a time to be moving. When pupils are asked to create (or recreate) a series of 'Still Images' (Section 5.12), they are usually asked to transition between the images in slow motion.

2 Using the strategies as 'thought and talk' frames

Many of the 'drama' strategies can be intentionally used as 'thought and talk' frames. The strategy that a teacher selects and the instructions that the teacher gives to the class can be varied to stimulate and scaffold different types of thinking and talk. Professor Robin Alexander (2017a) clearly recognises the particular significance of improvised drama, in relation to the range of pupils' thinking and talking together.

> Children's capacities to use talk to reason, argue, explain, explore, justify, challenge, question, negotiate, speculate, imagine, evaluate, ... to take ownership of their talking and thinking ... is actually not unlike ... the kind of discussion that might be generated to support and explore improvised drama.
>
> Alexander (2017, page 5)

The names of some strategies directly link to thought and talk, such as 'Thought-tracking' (Section 5.18), 'Conscience Alley' (Section 5.19), 'Thought-walk' (Section 5.23), 'Passing Thoughts' (Section 5.24), 'Thought Collage' (Section 5.33), 'Eavesdropping' (Section 5.5), 'Rumours' (Section 5.7), and 'Voice Collage' (Section 5.32). Strategies are continuously evolving over time, and some have acquired several names. 'Eavesdropping' is also referred to as 'overheard conversations', and a 'Conscience Alley' is sometimes called a 'Decision Alley' (Section 5.20), a 'Thought Tunnel' (Section 5.21), or a 'Corridor of Voices' (Section 5.22). Changes in terminology may indicate a shift in the way that the strategy is being used and adapted in practice by some teachers. In a 'Conscience Alley', the pupils voice the conflicting thoughts that are going on within a character's conscience. In a 'Decision Alley', the voices in the opposite lines are persuading a character towards making - or not making - a particular decision (which, of course, may be a matter of conscience). A 'Corridor of Voices' suggests greater flexibility, in terms of the talk expectations and need not be primarily focused on persuasive speech. These strategies (and others) not only stimulate and encourage individual pupils to think, they also invite and enable them to think and talk together, i.e. to interthink (Mercer, 2000).

> By using spoken language, people are able to think productively and creatively together. We call this process 'interthinking' to emphasise that people do not use talk only to inter*act*, they inter*think*'.
>
> Littleton and Mercer (2013, page 1, emphasis in original)

Teachers can – and should – feel free to adapt the strategies for their own classes and learning purposes. They can vary their instructions to shift the thought and talk opportunities and expectations. For example, during a 'Corridor of Voices', the pupils could be asked to offer one piece of information to the character as he/she passes by, or to speak something reassuring to the character, or just make a comment about the character as they pass, etc. If teachers ask pupils to include the word 'because', this will lead them into justifying and explaining what they are saying.

Internal monologue

A 'Thought-walk' (Section 5.23) gives pupils the opportunity to say out loud to themselves what they are thinking and feeling at a particular moment. It helps them clarify their individual thoughts and speak them out loud, with nobody listening (at least initially). Afterwards, they might be asked to share their thinking with others, in which case the 'Thought-walk' will have functioned as a form of rehearsal. 'Thought-walking' can be about anything, including current issues, e.g. artificial intelligence (AI), migration, or climate change. Pupils can be asked to 'Thought-walk' about an issue, immediately before participating in a class discussion about it.

'Thought-tracking' (Section 5.18) also gives pupils the opportunity to share their individual thoughts aloud, but usually briefly, and at a moment that is signalled (usually by the teacher). During 'Passing Thoughts' (Section 5.24), the pupils decide for themselves, whether and when to share a brief thought with the class, whilst they are walking across a class circle.

Dialogue

Dialogue is a conversation between two or more people. In drama, the conversation is often happening in role, within an imaginary context, and might be improvised, devised, or script-based. Various strategies stimulate and invite spontaneous dialogue, e.g. 'Telephone Conversations' (Section 5.38) offer an opportunity for an improvised dialogue between two people who are sitting back to back. 'Rumours' (Section 5.7) get pupils moving around and having improvised conversations with each other. 'Small Group Playmaking' (Section 5.15) usually starts with an out of role dialogue, during which pupils share their ideas and plan a group scene, then go on to rehearse and present their devised scene, which usually includes a dialogue in role. Meetings involve dialogue (Section 5.3), formal and/or informal. A 'Teacher-in-Role' (Section 5.2) can have conversations with pupils in roles that are far beyond the usual teacher-pupil dialogues, in terms of language, content, and style.

Questioning

'Hot-seating' (Section 5.17) is a familiar and commonly used strategy. The class can talk with and question someone who is on the hot-seat. Teachers can intentionally use this strategy to help improve and develop their pupils' questioning skills.

Teachers can allow an unrehearsed stream of spontaneous questions or might prefer to restrict the number of questions that any individual pupil (or group of pupils) can ask.

16 *Using the strategies as 'thought and talk' frames*

Limiting the number, types, and time for questions usually gets the class thinking more carefully about the questions they ask and can help prevent the same few pupils from asking most of the questions.

Teachers might say that nobody can ask more than two questions in a row, unless the second question directly follows on from the answer given to the first question,

Teachers might sometimes require pupils to ask different types of questions, perhaps at different stages of the 'hot-seating' process. For example, initial questions might have to be for clarification purposes only before pupils are invited to move on to more open questions, as happens during action learning (Revans, 1998).

Teachers might ask pupils to come up with questions in pairs or small groups, talk about their questions together, and decide which most need to be asked (as time will be limited). Together, they will be selecting, prioritising, and refining their questions.

The class might sometimes be asked to write their questions on self-adhesive labels and display them collectively on a flipchart. The person being hot-seated might be invited to choose which questions to answer or be invited to decide the order in which they answer the questions.

Teachers can join in and ask questions, too, modelling good questioning and focusing the pupils' attention in certain areas and directions. High-quality questioning usually leads to deeper thinking – for the questioner, for the person answering the question, and for those listening to both the questions and answers.

During drama lessons, the person on the hot-seat is usually answering 'in role' – but they need not necessarily be; e.g. in an English lesson, the person on the hot-seat might be answering questions about a book they have read. In a History lesson, a group of pupils might give a short presentation about something they have been learning about and researching, e.g. mummification. After presenting, they can be open to answering questions from the class. Any questions they are unable to answer can be noted for further enquiry, or the teacher might wish to answer the question.

Descriptive talk

Thinking and talking descriptively can stimulate the imagination and trigger multi-sensory memories. Teachers can select and set up strategies to specifically focus and stimulate pupils to talk descriptively (and sometimes cumulatively) about real or imaginary characters and creatures, real or fictional landscapes, and settings, situations and events (for example).

The class may have been reading about a fictional setting or creature within a story in English, and can be asked to imagine they are eyewitnesses, all present, looking at the same scene and describing it aloud, e.g. describing the Minotaur and/or the labyrinth. They might even be asked to physically become parts of the setting and/or monster and describe themselves verbally, 'in role' (see 'Talking Objects', Section 5.42 and '3D Landscapes', Section 5.41).

In History, Art, Geography, and PSHE and Relationships Education, a class might be shown paintings, photographs, or films which they can be asked to describe 'as if' they are present at the scene as eyewitnesses (Section 5.6). They may be asked to use sentence stems when speaking descriptively (and maybe cumulatively), in turn, e.g. 'I can see . . .', 'I can hear . . .', or 'I can smell . . .'. Talking descriptively – 'as if' they are present at the scene – can be particularly engaging, stimulating and motivational.

Cumulative talk

During cumulative talk, pupils need to accept and build on whatever others have already said. Various strategies stimulate and invite cumulative talk, e.g. 'Collective Role' (Section 5.30), when they each speak sequentially; 'as if' they are a single character talking; and 'Decision Alley' (Section 5.20), when pupils in a line cumulatively and sequentially persuade a character towards making a particular decision.

Strategies can be selected that verbally share class knowledge in any curriculum lesson. For example, a 'Corridor of Voices' (Section 5.22) or 'Passing Thoughts' (Section 5.24) can be set up in such a way that the pupils cumulatively add something that each knows about a geographical location, a current issue, or an historical character or event (for example). The protocols associated with such strategies help ensure that everyone listens to each other and gets the opportunity to be listened to.

Persuasive speech

Pupils need to talk persuasively to characters who pass by them in a 'Conscience Alley' (Section 5.19) or a 'Decision Alley' (Section 5.20). It is usually the teacher who walks through the alley, and the teacher can choose to linger longer by certain pupils, to give some pupils longer than others, to talk increasingly persuasively.

Whole class improvisations can be set up that specifically require persuasive speech, linked to various areas of the curriculum. For example, the teacher might take on the role of king and the class might be in 'Collective Role' (Section 5.30) as Samuel Pepys, trying to persuade King Charles II to instruct the Mayor of London to knock down houses and create a fire break (Baldwin and Galaska, 2022), or the class might try persuading King Henry VIII not to behead Ann Boleyn. In environmental education, they might be trying to persuade the boss of a logging company to stop chopping down trees in the Amazonian rainforest (Baldwin and Hendy, 1994). In a PSHE and Relationships lesson, they might try persuading an imaginary thief (the 'Teacher-in-Role', Section 5.2) to give back something they have stolen. They might first do some enquiry-based learning to be well informed when engaged in their persuasive arguments.

Exploratory talk

Many of the strategies meet some (or all) the criteria of 'exploratory talk' (Mercer, 2008), which encourage everyone to contribute and actively listen to each other. All opinions and ideas are actively listened to and treated with respect, and questions get asked. Relevant information is shared within an atmosphere of mutual trust, and the class tries to reach agreement.

Stories (and improvised, whole class drama), often are based on a fictional community that has to deal with realistic problems of some sort, e.g. migrants arriving on the local beach, a plague of rats, a foolish king, an historical plague, hostile invaders from another country, etc. When pupils become actively and collaboratively engaged with a fiction, they will usually start thinking of ways to solve the problems together, and during this process, they will be using 'exploratory talk'.

Devising group presentations or scenes together certainly requires 'exploratory talk'. The group need to generate and listen to each other's ideas; share, discuss, and explore possibilities for inclusion in the presentation/scene; and give reasons, explanations, and justifications for rejecting some ideas and selecting others for development. Group members will question each other. The presentation or scene that is being developed will need to be jointly evaluated, and ways of refining and improving it need to be discussed and agreement reached before the presentation or scene is finally presented or performed to the rest of the class.

Accountable talk

Accountable talk (Resnick et al., 2018) can take place in real or imagined worlds teachers (in or out of role), can present the class with realistic challenges and problems to think about and discuss in collaborative, solution-focused ways, e.g. family and friendship difficulties, or matters of community or global concern. The teacher can use various strategies to facilitate the 'thought and talk' process, e.g. 'Passing Thoughts' (Section 5.24), but the pupils are accountable for the information they give, the positions they take, and the statements they make. They need to be able to justify, reason, and explain any claims and statements they make, e.g. see 'Spectrum of Difference/Spectrogram' (Section 5.26) and 'Proxemics' (Section 5.25). They must also be open to being challenged and questioned (see 'Hot-seating', Section 5.17) and be willing to consider counterclaims, alternatives, and other people's viewpoints and positions. They also need to be willing to reflect on their own reasoning and perhaps change their minds about their initial statement and claims.

When 'Mantle of the Expert' (Section 5.4) is used (Heathcote and Bolton, 1995), pupils are often talking accountably to each other, 'as if' they are task-oriented professionals of some sort. They will also be using accountable talk when meeting with the external client who has commissioned the work from them (probably the 'Teacher-in-Role').

Sentence stems

Teachers can ask pupils to use specific sentence stems at various times. They will prompt different types of thought and talk. For example, when studying a photograph or painting, they might be asked to start sentences with, 'I notice' (observational) and then move on to 'I wonder' (possibility). After reading a text or 'hot-seating' a character, the class might be asked to voice sentences that start with 'I know . . .' (referential) then move on to 'I think I know . . .' (inferential) and finish with 'I want to know . . .' (enquiry).

Examples of sentence stems include the following.

> I notice . . .
> I wonder . . .
> I know . . .
> I think I know . . .
> I want to know . . .
> I hope . . .
> I expect . . .
> In my opinion, . . .
> I predict . . .
> I used to think . . .
> I now realise . . .
> On reflection, . . .
> Others may think . . .
> I think . . .
> This is important because . . .

When teachers ask pupils to include the word 'because', it prompts explanation, justification, and reasoning, e.g. 'In my opinion, the school should not make us have a new school uniform *because* lots of families can't afford to buy a different uniform' or 'I think we should have a new school uniform because the one we've got now looks really old fashioned'.

Disputational talk

Using strategies to explore and resolve fictional – yet realistic – disputes can be helpful when teaching PSHE and Relationships Education. If pupils are working in role, it is the fictional character who is involved in the dispute, and not the pupil themself. When they come out of role, they leave the fictional character behind and can then reflect objectively with the class about the scene.

Freezing a scene that is underway and contains a dispute (see 'Freeze-frame', Section 5.11) then enables that scene to be kept still for a while and reflected on (either in and/or out of role) before continuing the scene, or perhaps rewinding and replaying it differently, as happens during Boal's Forum Theatre (Boal, 2019).

A 'Conscience Alley' (Section 5.19) provides a structure for contributing to and hearing opposing viewpoints, perhaps prior to a discussion. 'Thought-tracking' (Section 5.18) enables a class to hear characters' inner thoughts, which may be at odds with what they are saying publicly. 'Proxemics' (Section 5.25) and 'Spectrum of Difference/Spectrogram' (Section 5.26) are all strategies that enable everyone to see where people stand on given issues, both literally and metaphorically. Repeating these strategies at different times sometimes reveals that some have people have changed their positions.

Presentational talk

Presentations are for an audience and can be seen as a type of performance. They require the speaker to have an awareness of their audience throughout, and to speak and 'act' clearly and confidently. Presentations are usually prepared, illustrated, and rehearsed. It can be helpful for pupils to 'pretend' that they are talking to an imaginary audience, in advance of talking to a real audience (usually their class). Their presentations could be about some aspect of their work in any curriculum area. Within drama lessons, presentations are sometimes given in role, within a fictional context, e.g. when 'Mantle of the Expert' (Section 5.4) is being used, the pupils might be presenting their ideas or outcomes to each other and/or to an external client (probably their 'Teacher-in-Role', Section 5.2).

Debate

Debate involves at least two speakers, both formally presenting the opposing sides of an argument in an organised and well-informed way. Those who are listening usually end up being asked to vote for one side or the other. A 'Corridor of Voices' (Section 5.22) can be used to help a speaker gather some relevant points for possible inclusion in their presentation. A 'Decision Alley' (Section 5.20) can be used to get the main opposing points of each side reiterated (perhaps just before voting takes place). The statement being debated and then voted on, could be subject-specific, cross-curricular, and/or issue-based, e.g. 'AI is a force for good' or 'Dogs should not be allowed on beaches in summer months'.

Informative speech

Some strategies provide a structure for the giving and/or gathering of information. For example, during a 'Corridor of Voices' (Section 5.22), the teacher can ask the pupils to only give information and not offer opinions. The information gathered can then be used when devising a subsequent presentation. When pupils are being asked to talk informatively, they can be asked to use a sentence stem such as, 'I know . . .'.

In drama lessons, pupils are sometimes asked to give information about scenes that they have witnessed. They might be imparting information in role, perhaps telling a curious friend or an investigative journalist (probably the 'Teacher-in-Role', Section 5.2), for example. Information that is gathered about characters can be recorded on a 'Role on the Wall' (Section 5.29).

'Information giving' is often one of the main functions of a 'Teacher-in-Role' (Section 5.2), e.g. the teacher could be in role as Howard Carter, talking at a press conference about what has been found in Tutankhamun's tomb (Baldwin, 2008). The pupils might be in role as investigative journalists, listening first and then asking questions before writing a newspaper report.

Justification and explanation

Pupils can be asked to explain and justify their positioning, for example, in relation to a character, idea, statement, or issue (see 'Spectrum of Difference/Spectrogram', Section 5.26 and 'Proxemics', Section 5.25). When using these strategies to get pupils justifying and explaining their positions, they are usually asked to start their sentences with, 'I am standing here because . . .'. The idea, statement, issue, or the character is placed in the centre of a class circle, and the pupils enter in turn and position themselves in relation to it, justifying and explaining their relative positioning. This helps them to know and get to understand each other's positions, maybe leading into a discussion or debate, following which some pupils may have shifted their positions if the strategies are subsequently repeated. If they do change positions, they can be asked to justify and explain the change, starting with, 'I have now changed my position because . . .'.

Listening

Listening is a skill, and both teachers and pupils need to develop it and need to be actively listened to themselves. The strategies each have protocols that make clear when pupils may talk and when they need to be listening to each other. For strategies to work effectively, their protocols need to be followed. For example, during 'Rumours' (Section 5.7) and 'Eavesdropping' (Section 5.5), the pupils need to listen to each other in order to be able to gather information that can be repeated and elaborated on. When improvising, they need to listen carefully to what others are saying in order to be able to respond appropriately. When devising short scenes and presentations, they need to listen to each other's ideas, to respond to them, to ask appropriate questions, and to give constructive feedback. Pupils also need to listen carefully to analyse and take on board critical feedback they may receive. In many subject lessons (and certainly in drama lessons), there are times when pupils' speech and actions are being clearly directed, so they need to listen carefully in order to follow the directions. When pupils are questioning someone, they must listen to the answers or there will have been little point in asking the question. A response given to a question can influence the next question. During a 'Conscience Alley' (Section 5.19), everyone needs to listen to what is being said to avoid repetition. When participating in a 'Voice Collage' (Section 5.32), 'Thought Collage' (Section 5.33), or 'Sound Collage' (Section 5.34), everyone needs to listen to each other, to judge the moments when it will be most effective for them to join in vocally. When pupils are talking cumulatively as a single character, they need to avoid repetition and ensure there is continuity and consistency evident, in what is being said (see 'Collective Role', Section 5.30).

Equal opportunities to talk

In 'Passing Thoughts' (Section 5.24), pupils can decide when, whether, and how often to walk across the circle and speak. They all have equal opportunity to speak but some pupils may choose to hold back, whilst others might take several turns (although the teacher might decide to restrict the total number of turns any pupil can have).

To ensure that all pupils get a turn at sharing their thoughts with the class, an object such as a shell or stick can be passed around a class circle ritualistically. Whoever is holding the object may speak without being interrupted, and everyone else is expected to listen and await their turn. When the pupil holding the object finishes speaking, they pass it on to the next pupil in the circle. Pupils can decide not to take their turn to speak, in which case, they just silently pass the object on. Objects are often used in this way during 'Circle Time'.

Varying the pace of talk

Several drama strategies get pupils thinking out loud, but the pace at which thoughts are shared sometimes varies between strategies. During a 'Conscience Alley' (Section 5.19), it is the person walking between the lines (usually the teacher) who sets the pace. During 'Passing Thoughts', each pupil decides how quickly they will cross the circle and speak, and during a 'Voice Collage' (Section 5.32) or 'Thought Collage' (Section 5.33), the pace and volume of the pupils' voices can either be conducted or directed by the teacher or left for the pupils to judge once the strategy is underway.

3 Using the strategies to support and improve writing

Focusing strategies towards writing

Many strategies can be set up to stimulate different types of talk as preparation for pupils carrying out different types of writing, individually and/or collaboratively. Various strategies can be framed so that pupils start generating and sharing appropriate words, phrases, sentences, questions, descriptions, etc., that can then be jotted down, gathered, and used as a class resource bank during the subsequent writing task.

When a teacher has a specific type of writing task in mind, it is likely to influence their choice of strategy and the instructions they give to the pupils when setting it up. They need to get their pupils talking in specific ways – e.g. descriptively, persuasively, or informatively – to appropriately support the linked writing task that will follow.

Stories and story-dramas

Stories have been told universally since ancient times and can be used to entertain, give information, and pass on cultural knowledge and values. Before stories were written down, they were repeatedly told, sometimes altered, and often accompanied by dramatic gestures and re-enactments.

History, religions, cultures, places, and communities worldwide all have significant stories, which have been recorded in writing. True and fictional stories contain characters, settings, plots, situations, problems, tensions, dilemmas, pivotal moments, challenging situations, and events, many of which can be (or already are) recorded and documented in different ways by different writers, often from a range of viewpoints and for different purposes and audiences.

Strategies can be used to get pupils interactively and collaboratively engaging with any true or fictional story, as well as creating their own stories individually and/or collaboratively. When pupils enter stories together in role, (maybe with their 'Teacher-in-Role', too), they start experiencing the story in an interactive way, which can deepen their engagement and understanding of the story. Strategies enable them to meet and become the characters in any story, actively imagine themselves to be present within the story's settings, and become socially, emotionally, physically, and cognitively engaged with plots.

Having a reason to write during a story-drama is usually more motivating for pupils than just writing about the story afterwards. When pupils are working in role together within an

DOI: 10.4324/9781003343080-4

imaginary context, their writing can become necessary, e.g. they might need to write a joint letter to their misguided king, or write an secret diary entry, or write a newspaper report about something that has happened in the story-drama. When pupils feel that their writing is purposeful and they are writing for a responsive reader/audience that is present (maybe their 'Teacher-in-Role', or other pupils in role), they are often highly motivated to write and the writing often improves.

Various strategies can help bring scenes from stories to life (see 'Small Group Playmaking', Section 5.15). Groups can be asked to devise and mime a scene, with others providing an accompanying narrative, i.e. by 'talking like a writer'. They can devise additional scenes for known stories, present and narrate them, then write them up as playscripts or write them up 'in the style' of the original author and seamlessly insert them into the original text.

Teachers can model 'talking like a writer' when engaged in 'Active Storytelling' (Section 5.9), 'Whoosh!' (Section 5.10), or 'Teacher as Storyteller' (Section 5.8). Listening to and watching good storytelling will help pupils to develop their own storytelling skills, and this can be of benefit to their story writing.

3D story-boarding for writing

Any true or fictitious story can be presented chronologically, as a sequence of devised 'Still Images' (Section 5.12), or as a series of short scenes (see 'Small Group Playmaking', Section 5.15), then can be shared through a 'Performance Carousel' (Section 5.16). A series of images or scenes can be used as a three-dimensional (3D) storyboard to guide the pupils' narrative writing of the story afterwards. Each image or scene in the sequence could become the basis of a paragraph or chapter subsequently written by the pupils.

Comics and graphic novels tell stories through a series of still images. The characters' thoughts are often written within thought bubbles, and their speech within speech bubbles. The depicted scenes often also have captions written below them. When pupils devise and present a series of 'Still Images' (Section 5.12), they can be asked to each speak a sentence or thought in role as a character within the image (see 'Thought-tracking', Section 5.18). Series of 'still images' can be photographed, and speech bubbles, thought bubbles, and captions then added.

Different viewpoints, purposes, and audiences for writing

Scenes can be told and then written in different forms, for various purposes and audiences, and from different character's viewpoints. For example, in a scene in which a crime is committed (see 'Small Group Playmaking', Section 5.15), questions might be put to victims, suspects, and eyewitnesses (see 'Hot-seating', Section 5.17). Notes need to be taken. Those asking the questions might be in role as police officers or journalists. After the interview, they may need to write police reports or newspaper reports. An eyewitness, victim, or suspect might be asked to write a formal statement for the police. Alternatively, or additionally, an eyewitness or victim might write about the incident informally, in an email or letter to a friend, or in their personal diary.

Teachers as co-writers, commissioning editors, and non-writers

Teachers in role can work alongside their pupils in role, as co-writers of equal status, with a specific writing task to complete together. Alternatively, teachers might position themselves in role as the scribe for their pupils in role. As a scribe, the teacher can guide and share the writing throughout the writing process from within the role. Teachers might sometimes choose to adopt a higher-status role, such as a commissioning editor, with their pupils in role as professional writers with a task to complete. When using 'Mantle of the Expert' (Section 5.4), pupils are usually commissioned by an imaginary external client (usually the 'Teacher-in-Role') to complete certain tasks for them, and these can include writing tasks. For example, if the pupils are in role as 'expert' museum curators, they might be primarily tasked with designing a museum exhibition about Ancient Egypt. However, their work might include having to write information labels for each exhibit, an exhibition catalogue, and/or a poster and flyer advertising the exhibition. There would be a specific purpose and audience for their writing, and they would have deadlines to meet.

A teacher might decide to adopt a low-status role, maybe as someone who cannot read or write. They can then ask the pupils to help them to write something important, e.g. a letter of apology or a witness statement. The pupils know that their teacher can write but the class will go along with the pretence and want to help. They need to question the 'Teacher-in-Role' as to the required content of the writing, its purpose, and its intended audience. They need to listen carefully, take notes, then draft what is required, read it to the 'Teacher-in-Role', probably make some changes, and finally give the completed piece of writing to the grateful 'Teacher-in-Role'.

Character studies

Information gathered about characters (real or fictitious) can be jotted onto self-adhesive labels and stuck around an outline of the character, (see 'Role on the Wall', Section 5.29). This can be done individually or collaboratively. A series of 'roles on the wall' for a character can be completed at different moments in time and used later if pupils are writing a character study.

From 'page to stage' and 'stage to page'

Pupils often use writing frames to help them organise their thoughts before they start writing. They sometimes jot down possible words and phrases that they might use. Writing frames sometimes have headed sections and can include sentence stems for completion. Anything that pupils jot down on a writing frame can be verbally presented on a stage area which has been divided into headed sections that replicate those on the writing frame. In turn, each pupil can enter a Section of the stage and 'perform' a sentence or phrase that fits there. Conversely, teachers could ask pupils to perform sentences and phrases on the sectioned stage first, and then jot them down afterwards on paper writing frames.

What is said by the two lines of opposing voices during a 'Conscience Alley' (Section 5.19) or 'Decision Alley' (Section 5.20) can be jotted down afterwards in two separately headed columns, e.g. pros and cons. This resource can then be referred to if pupils are asked to write a persuasive or balanced argument. Conversely, pupils can start by writing the pros and cons of a course of action (under headed columns) and then stage what they have written, 'as if' the stage is divided into columns and they have an imaginary audience listening and watching.

Thought bubbles and speech bubbles

Various strategies invite pupils to speak thoughts aloud, e.g. 'Thought-tracking' (Section 5.18), 'Passing Thoughts' (Section 5.24), 'Thought-walk' (Section 5.23), and 'Thought Tunnel' (Section 5.21). Afterwards, each voiced thought can be jotted onto on a self-adhesive thought bubble. The thoughts can then be gathered, displayed, and used as a class resource for subsequent writing, e.g. when writing about what the locals thought when they found a migrant and his raft on the local beach, as happens in *The Island*, a picture book by Armin Greder (2002).

Pupils can be invited to think aloud in turn, 'as if' they are all the same character (see 'Collective Role' (Section 5.30). Each thought can then be jotted down on a self-adhesive label and the thoughts can then be collected and displayed then used as a central resource for writing a soliloquy. 'Collective Role' (Section 5.30) can also be used to gather the public utterances of a single character and these can be written on speech bubbles then collected and displayed. Sometimes, the thought bubbles and speech bubbles from a single character might be compared, and this might reveal that what a character is thinking to themselves is not congruent with what they are saying publicly, e.g. Judas Iscariot at the Last Supper.

Drafting on the move

Before writing a diary entry (in role), pupils could be asked to first carry out a 'Thought-walk' (Section 5.23). They will be talking aloud to themselves about whatever they are thinking and feeling, maybe about a character, situation, event, dilemma, topic, or issue, for example. They could also be asked to 'Thought-walk' (Section 5.23) before writing a letter to someone. The 'walk and talk' gives a verbal flow of possible content, which can then be selected from and refined by the pupil both before and during their subsequent writing.

Objects and settings can talk and write

Inanimate objects and artefacts can come to life and talk about themselves and their experiences (see 'Talking Objects', Section 5.42). They can tell others about their personal histories, the journeys they have been taken on, scenes they have eyewitnessed, and conversations they have overheard. What objects and artefacts say can be noted and used to inform a personified, first-person recount (i.e. using 'I', 'we', 'our', and/or 'my') or a third person recount (i.e. using 'their', 'they', 'he', or 'she'). Objects can also answer questions about their owners (see 'Hot-seating', Section 5.17), and the information they give about them can be jotted around a 'Role on the Wall' (Section 5.29) and be helpful if pupils are writing a character study.

Inanimate settings can also become animated. When pupils are in role 'as if' they are different parts of the same setting, they can in turn, speak descriptively about themselves (see '3D Landscapes', Section 5.41). What the setting says can be jotted down, gathered, and used if pupils are asked to write a description of the setting afterwards. Settings can also answer questions and can recount who and what they have seen and heard at various times. With younger pupils, the teacher needs to consider whether it would be more appropriate for a teaching assistant to jot down what the pupils say. The subsequent writing might be done individually but could be done collaboratively, with the teacher as facilitator.

'Making sense' of settings

Pupils can lead their 'blind' partners on a 'Sensory Journey' (Section 5.37) through imaginary settings. One pupil closes their eyes and the other leads them on an imaginary journey through the setting (maybe by the arm). The guide tries to describe for their partner what can supposedly be seen, heard, smelt, touched, and maybe tasted as they move together through the setting. The guide works hard at describing the setting, and this helps the 'blind' partner imagine the place but may also help the guide – if they go on afterwards – to write about the imaginary setting and journey. Usually, both pupils get a turn at being the guide and the guided.

Whole classes can be asked to close their eyes and imagine they are together in the same setting. Their teacher can start talking in a multi-sensory and descriptive way about the imagined surroundings and then invite the class to join in and descriptively add further details. The pupils might be asked to use multi-sensory sentence stems, e.g. 'I can see . . .', 'I can hear . . .', etc. This collaborative activity can be used prior to the class writing descriptively about the setting.

Mapping settings

Maps of fictional settings can be made which are linked to stories the class has read or stories that they are going to create together and write. Maps can be drawn collaboratively, working either in or out of role, see 'Story Maps' (Section 5.40). The maps might show landscape features, important buildings, and places of personal and communal significance to the who live in the area represented on the map.

Once the map is finished, the class can stand either side of it (with each pupil standing near whatever they added to the map). The teacher can then walk slowly along the map, from one end to the other (perhaps with their eyes closed). As the 'blind' teacher passes by each pupil in turn, the pupil needs to vividly describe what they have added to the map to help the passer-by visualise it, e.g. 'You are passing the old, cold, stone church. Its graveyard is overgrown'. Alternatively, the class can be asked to use the poetic literary device of personification, and speak 'as if' they are whatever they have added to the map, e.g. 'I am the old, cold stone church. My graveyard is overgrown'. By the time the teacher reaches the end of the map, everyone will have gained quite a lot of information about the place they have just created together and about the imaginary community that lives there (which they might then belong to in a subsequent story-drama).

The pupils can write and add labels, sentences, or even paragraphs to the map, sticking them next to whatever they have each contributed to it. The map will prove to be a useful resource for the class if they are subsequently asked to write about the place on the map and perhaps the community of people who live there. The map is a central resource that can be further developed and annotated as more becomes known about the place and the people who live there, maybe through 'Improvisation' (Section 5.1) and/or 'Small Group Playmaking' (Section 5.15).

Alternative, additional, and altered texts

Moments, scenes, and events that are being described and recounted in any type of published text can be illustrated using 'Still Images' (Section 5.12) and then brought to life through 'Improvisation' (Section 5.1) and/or 'Small Group Playmaking' (Section 5.15). Dialogue may be generated during the process that does not appear in the original text, and it can be written up afterwards in the form of a short playscript.

Additional scenes can be devised, added, presented, or performed and then written and inserted seamlessly into the original text, almost 'as if' they were written by the original author. For example, a class might be reading and actively exploring the poem 'The Pied Piper of Hamelin' by Robert Browning. The poem contains various examples of the problems being caused by a plague of rats, e.g. biting babies, loud squeaking, etc. In groups, the class can be asked to come up with other possible rat-related incidents that are not mentioned in Browning's poem. Groups can devise and present their additional rat incidents as 'still images' (Section 5.12), or as short scenes (see 'Small Group Playmaking', Section 5.15). They can then go back to the poem, remove one of Browning's incidents, and substitute one of their own instead, 'as if' Browning had written it (Baldwin, 2019). They will need to use the same style, rhythm, and meter as the original text, and groups might then be invited to read the changed verses aloud.

Once pupils are familiar with a narrative, they can be asked to recount it to a partner, 'as if' they are one of the characters in it. They can be asked to recount events, as if they happened recently or long ago. Verbally recounting a narrative in role can precede writing in role as that character, e.g. a formal or informal letter, a diary entry, etc. Writing in role can be carried out individually or collaboratively in pairs, in groups, or even as a whole class. For example, a class might be actively exploring Wilfred Owen's war poem 'Dulce et Decorum Est' and may have recreated its imagery physically ('Still Images', Section 5.12) or mimed the poem as it was being read aloud by the teacher ('Active Storytelling', Section 5.9). With the images still in their minds, the class might then be asked to collaboratively write a letter home from an injured soldier who has lived through the scenes they depicted from Owen's poem. A single letter could be written by the class (or groups), using 'Collective Role' (Section 5.30). The teacher could be in role, too, throughout the process as a guide and scribe. Each pupil could in turn be asked to add one sentence to the letter (which would have then been censored). Alternatively, the pupils could be in role as the soldier, writing an uncensored recount of the same wartime experiences, but many years later, after the war has ended.

4 Using the strategies to make and explore images

Images are used in the teaching of most curriculum subjects, particularly the arts and humanities. Some 'drama' strategies focus on the construction, reconstruction, and exploration of still and/or moving images. They enable pupils to make and/or explore images in various ways, and from different viewpoints. Strategies can be selected that help pupils think about images, individually and/or together, in relation to the content, composition, significance, and meaning of any image, two- or three-dimensional, still or moving.

Images that pupils form individually or collaboratively with their bodies can be formed, reformed, transformed, added to, and/or extended. Embodying an image helps make it more memorable and can also make any associated learning become more memorable.

History

In lessons, pupils might be shown historic film footage, simulations, paintings, photographs, tapestries, carvings, and statues, for example. Any of these forms of image can be replicated, using 'Still Images' (Section 5.12) and brought to life using 'Improvisation' (Section 5.1) or 'Small Group Playmaking' (Section 5.15).

Historic photographs and film clips can be projected onto a wall and the pupils can be invited to join the scene for a while, 'as if' they are present 'in the moment' as invisible eyewitnesses. They can be invited to comment aloud about what they can see, e.g. when looking at the objects inside Tutankhamun's recently opened tomb (Baldwin, 2008). Pupils can become the people and/or the objects within an historic image (see 'Talking Objects', Section 5.42). They can talk in role from within the image, to each other (see 'Improvisation', Section 5.1) and/or to interested questioners (see 'Hot-seating', Section 5.17).

English

Picture books, illustrated texts, and graphic novels, all contain images that can be physically replicated as 'Still Images' (Section 5.12). These can then come to life for a while (see 'Improvisation', Section 5.1). The characters within images can be invited to think aloud (see 'Thought-tracking' (Section 5.18) and maybe answer questions, either from within the image, or once they have stepped out of it for a while (see 'Hot-seating', Section 5.17).

DOI: 10.4324/9781003343080-5

Alternative and/or additional 'still images' (Section 5.12) can be formed that appropriately illustrate various parts of the text. Groups of pupils might even be asked to physically devise a new image for the cover for the book. They can be asked to devise images, depicting what might happen next in a story, or to devise an image that depicts an alternative ending. Image making is an embodied, collaborative learning experience. The groups need to discuss and agree what they most want to communicate through their image, and then create an image that effectively achieves this.

Written text often contains strong, visual imagery. Teachers can draw the attention of the pupils to the visual imagery in a text by asking them to walk around the room until the teacher calls out an example of visual imagery from within the text, e.g. 'My bounty is as boundless as the sea/My love as deep' (Shakespeare's Juliet says this to Romeo) or, 'O that this too too solid flesh would melt, Thaw, and resolve itself into a dew' (Hamlet). The pupils then immediately respond by miming something appropriately, until the teacher calls out, 'Move on'. After a while, the teacher calls out another example from the text, and so on.

Teachers can ask pupils to underline any examples of visual imagery that they find within a given text. Then in pairs or groups, they can physically form some of the imagery, using movement, mime, or still images.

Geography

In Geography lessons, classes often study photographs and film clips of the places and people that they are learning about. Authentic images can be projected on to a wall and the pupils can be asked to say what they can see, 'as if' they are professionals observing and interpreting the place and its people (see 'Mantle of the Expert', Section 5.4). They can be asked to use specific sentence stems such as, 'I notice . . .' and then, 'I wonder . . .'. These sentence stems can encourage careful observation, interpretation, and speculation.

In Geography, young children start to learn about maps and may be introduced to then through aerial views. Teachers can take their classes on imaginary hot-air balloon rides as a stimulus for map-making together afterwards. Picture books and some other fictional texts may contain maps that relate to the story. These are often pictorial maps. Pupils can enter a space and physically become something that is on the map, stating what they are as they get into position, e.g. 'I am an old stone bridge. There is a troll living underneath me' (see '3D Landscapes', Section 5.41, 'Talking Objects', Section 5.42, and 'Drama Maps', Section 5.39).

Personal social health economic (PSHE) and Relationships Education

Teachers of PSHE and Relationships Education often use photographs, drawings, picture books, and film clips to initiate and focus discussions about personal and socially and emotionally challenging situations, e.g. conflicts between friends and within families. The class can be shown a photograph or film clip that shows a tense situation and/or conflict, for example, then talk together about it out of role in a safely distanced way. The teacher can then invite the pupils to talk with and advise the people within the scene. The teacher can then take on each of the roles in turn and the pupils can offer advice about ways of avoiding and resolving the conflict.

Groups of pupils can be asked to create a short scene, showing a typical problem developing during playtime. They can be asked to start their scene with a 'still image', bring it to life, then 'freeze' the scene at a pivotal moment (see 'Still Images', Section 5.12, 'Small Group Playmaking', Section 5.15, and 'Freeze-frame', Section 5.11). When devising the scene, the class will be considering how the problem starts and how it progresses towards the pivotal moment. Group scenes can be performed in turn and the class can talk with individual characters in the scenes and offer them advice about how to avoid, defuse, and/or resolve the problem that they have shown in their scene. The scenes could then be replayed differently, following the advice given (Baldwin and Galaska, 2022).

There are also many opportunities in PSHE and Relationships Education for physically devising and presenting pairs of images, i.e. 'the reality' and 'the ideal'. Having created a pair of contrasting images, the class can be asked to consider what the characters in the scene might need to do and say differently for them to move towards achieving 'the ideal' (Boal, 1995).

Art and Design

Art consists of two-dimensional (2D) images (such as a drawings, paintings, and photographs) and three-dimensional (3D) objects (such as a carvings and sculptures). 2D and 3D images can be physically devised or replicated, using strategies such as 'Still Images' (Section 5.12), '3D Landscapes' (Section 5.41), and 'Sculpting' (Section 5.13).

When young pupils are looking at pictures, the teacher could tell them that they are going to be 'picture detectives' and that they are particularly good at noticing the details in pictures that most people do not notice (see 'Mantle of the Expert', Section 5.4).

Pupils can physically replicate existing pieces of art or use their bodies to make their own original images (individually and/or together), which could subsequently be transposed into art. Depending on the level of pupils' knowledge and understanding, the images that the teacher asks them to make physically might be termed naturalistic, realistic, idealistic, symbolic, or abstract.

A triptych is a piece of artwork consisting of three images which are usually scenes painted on three separate panels that together convey a narrative, e.g. 'The Pioneer' (1904) by Frederick McCubbin. Groups of pupils can be asked to physically portray each image in turn, transitioning between each image in slow motion, and 'freezing' as each of the images for a while ('Freeze-frame', Section 5.11). To do this, they will need to first study the images carefully. Once they have embodied the images, they will be more memorable. Each of the images could come alive in turn for a while, using strategies such as 'Improvisation' (Section 5.1) or 'Small Group Playmaking' (Section 5.15). The characters in each image can be asked questions ('Hot-seating', Section 5.17), and their inner thoughts can be spoken ('Thought-tracking', Section 5.18). Additional panels can be devised as still images ('Still Images', Section 5.12) and inserted into the sequence of images. Pupils could even paint the missing images subsequently, 'in the style' of the original artist.

Triptychs do not always convey a narrative sequence. They sometimes convey the same subject matter, but in three different ways (which could be from the viewpoints of three different characters). Some triptychs are one image that has been split into three separate images.

Pupils can be presented with a single, projected image on the wall, then invited to create additional images physically on either side of the projected image (in effect, creating a tryptic).

Constructing, deconstructing, and melting images

Images can be constructed in various ways, including the following.

- When pairs, groups, or a class build a 'still image' (Section 5.12) together, the teacher might ask them to do so silently, with each person entering in turn, adding themselves to the growing image in some way, and then freezing in position.
- Alternatively, the teacher might give groups preparation time to discuss, negotiate, devise, and rehearse their image before they present it to the class.
- The 'Sculpting' (Section 5.13) strategy requires pupils to become physically malleable, 'as if' they are lumps of clay that allow themselves to be physically moulded (or verbally directed) by their partner, i.e. the 'sculptor'.

Images that have been assembled collectively are often dismantled in reverse order, with the last pupil who added themselves to the image being the first to withdraw from it. Alternatively, images can melt in slow motion, ending with everyone still on the floor.

Entering, elaborating on, and extending images

An image can be projected onto a wall, and pupils can be invited to do any of the following.

- Step forward in turn, enter the projected image, and position themselves as something (or somebody) that is already in the projected image.
- Enter the image in turn and add themselves to the image 'as if' they are something (or somebody) that is not already present in it.
- Enter in role and place themselves to the left or right of the projected image, thus extending it.
- Move closer to the image, in role as invisible eyewitnesses to the scene.

If the projected image is (for example) a photograph of wartime evacuees on a railway platform, or an overcrowded boat full of refugees, then the pupils might position themselves as one of the people in the photograph, or add more people, or become eyewitnesses of the scene. Such options need not only be used with projected images. If some pupils have already formed an image, then the teacher might invite other pupils to add themselves to it.

Contrasting images

Devising pairs of 'still images' can support learning in various subject areas. The first image can gradually be transformed into the second image to show contrast and/or how something has changed (or will change) over time, such as the following.

- The impact of humans on the environment, 'now and in the future' (Science and Geography).
- Transport 'then and now' (History).
- Lady Macbeth – 'awake and sleep walking' (English).
- The new boy's first day – 'the reality and the ideal' (PSHE and Relationships).

The process of devising pairs of contrasting images gets pupils thinking about possible content and discussing, negotiating, and deciding what needs to be included and what the changes in each of the images needs to be. They will hopefully provoke their audience to think deeply about the subject matter of the images, too.

Visualising images

Pupils can be asked to close their eyes and imagine a picture within their 'mind's eye'. The image the teacher asks them to imagine, for example, could be one of the following.

- A setting that they have all been reading about in a class text, e.g. Narnia (in *The Lion, The Witch and the Wardrobe* by C.S. Lewis).
- A setting that they have already seen (maybe in a picture book, in real life, or in a photograph).
- Their own original setting that they are now going to create collaboratively.

Whether working as a whole class, in pairs, or in groups, pupils can each be given the opportunity in turn to describe aloud something that they can see in their mind's eye that fits in with what others are visualising. They are all being guided to imagine that they are all present, in the same place. Such a visualisation might precede writing about a setting, mapping it, or entering it in role.

PART 2

5 The 'Drama' strategies

5.1 Improvisation

What it offers

'Improvisation' involves responding imaginatively and spontaneously to a stimulus, 'in the moment' and 'on the spot'. There is no time available for planning. When improvising, pupils are being invited – and expected – to respond quickly to whatever someone has just said and/or done. 'Improvisation' can sometimes involve responding creatively and interactively to an object, or whatever else is available.

When improvising, pupils are thinking creatively and practising responding to situations and stimuli, with confidence and at speed. What they are responding to might be fictional, far-fetched, or realistic. It may be a short or long improvisation. Whichever it is, the skills pupils bring to it will always be real.

'Improvisation' can be done individually or collaboratively. It is sometimes used by businesses and organisations for team-building and can be set up in such a way that the participants are using (and revealing), their work-related skills and abilities (e.g. confident and clear communication and presentation skills, creative thinking, problem-solving and leadership skills) and their willingness and ability to work collaboratively.

How to set it up

For improvisation to work well, everyone needs to be willing to contribute and help keep the improvisation going. Pupils need to watch and listen carefully to each other, accept whatever is given, react 'as if' it is real, and then quickly respond.

Very young children often improvise during dramatic play. They have unrehearsed conversations with toys, and make use of ambiguous objects 'as if' they were something else, e.g. a cardboard box might become a spaceship, a stick might be used as a sword, a piece of material might become a cloak, a small chair might become the seat of a car, etc. Passing such objects around a circle for each person to use imaginatively in turn is a well-known drama game.

Improvisations can commence with a simple 'set up' instruction from the teacher, e.g. a group might simply be asked to get into a line and imagine that they are standing at a bus

DOI: 10.4324/9781003343080-7

38 The 'Drama' strategies

stop together. Whatever happens next will be improvised by them. The teacher might decide to arrive at the bus stop too, and join in (see 'Teacher-in-Role', Section 5.2).

Pupils can be asked to improvise scenes that connect directly with subjects in and across the curriculum. They need to know who they are going to be in role as (their character), where they are (the setting), and what the situation is (plot). Various images and/or texts, available on the internet, can become the initial stimulus for an improvised crowd scene, such as the following.

- A photograph of parents on a railway platform, saying goodbye to their children as they are being evacuated during World War II (History).
- A photograph of the crowd on the quayside, watching the Titanic set off on her maiden voyage (History).
- The people of Hamelin, out on the streets talking together, just after the Pied Piper has got rid of the rats (English).
- The crowd standing on the wharf at Camelot, watching the dead Lady of Shalott float towards them (English).
- A photograph of an overcrowded boat of refugees (Current Affairs, PSHE and Relationships, Geography, Citizenship).

Just an opening sentence or two can be given to pairs of pupils, as a stimulus for 'Improvisation', such as the following.

> Pupil 1: You lied to me.
> Pupil 2: Yes, and I am sorry.
>
> Pupil 1: We must leave now.
> Pupil 2: But this is our home.
>
> Pupil 1: He threatened the new boy.
> Pupil 2: It's not our problem.

Conversely, pupils can be given the final sentence that their 'Improvisation' needs to end on, such as one of the following.

> Can we just stop talking about it?
> I'm going to tell the police.
> I've changed my mind.

Just a single word or phrase can be used as the stimulus for an 'Improvisation', such as one of the following.

> Help!
> Discovered.
> The final straw.
> The last goodbye.
> An act of kindness.

Teacher tips

- Start with some 'short improvisation' games and activities before moving on to 'long improvisation' and 'narrative improvisation' scenes.
- Do not let improvisations go on for longer than is purposeful and productive.
- Stress the importance of pupils accepting whatever they are given, staying in role throughout, and responding, 'as if' the scene is really happening now.
- Halt an improvisation if pupils are not staying in role and keeping it going. Then explain why you have halted the improvisation, and then let them try once more.

Linked activities

- Improvising with an ambiguous object, e.g. a chair, a stick, a box or a piece of material. This can be done individually, in pairs, in groups, or in class circles. These objects can also be passed around a class circle or placed in the centre, with each pupil in turn having the opportunity to improvise with the object.
- One pupil selects a random object, e.g. a stapler or box of pencils, and becomes a determined salesperson. They try to 'hard sell' the object to a customer, i.e. to their partner or the class.
- Pupils can improvise the telling of an original story together, with each person in turn adding one word, or one sentence, at a time until the story ends.
- One pupil in a pair, group, or class circle can start improvising a story. After a while, that pupil claps, which is the signal for the next person to carry on telling the same story. The story keeps being added to, then passed on with a clap, until the story ends.

5.2 Teacher-in-Role

What it offers

'Teacher-in-Role' is particularly effective when the teacher is clear about what they want the role to achieve for the pupils' learning. Pupils find their teacher working in role to be highly engaging and are often fascinated by this unusual type of pupil/teacher interaction.

Teachers might go into role for various learning and teaching purposes, such as the following.

- To give information, e.g. in role as Lord Shaftesbury, telling the government (the pupils) about child labour in coal mines (Baldwin and Hendy, 1994).
- To gather information from the pupils, e.g. as a newspaper reporter gathering their views on an issue of current concern such as worsening coastal erosion and the lack of sea defences.
- To deliver messages from a character who is not present, and/or take messages back to that character, e.g. as the Mayor of Hamelin's messenger (Baldwin, 2019).
- To introduce a problem or complication, e.g. to report that enemy ships have been seen, heading towards their shores.
- To ask for their help or advice, e.g. as the victim of an imaginary bully.
- To set a work-related task for the class, e.g. commissioning them to research and then create an art exhibition based on a specific artist, art movement, or theme.

Teachers can choose to take on roles of varying status. They might choose to adopt a role of equal status to that of their pupils, e.g. the teacher and pupils together are the townsfolk of Hamelin, and are being plagued by rats. The teacher could take on a lower status role, e.g. becoming a terrified refugee whose has landed on their shore. Teachers often take on high status roles, e.g. as a king whose new law is causing problems for everyone. Teachers in role may become intermediaries, e.g. the king's messenger. Intermediaries can be neutral and need not necessarily take any responsibility for the content of messages that they carry back and forth.

When teachers are in role, they can model appropriate ways of talking, behaving, and responding that fit with the imagined context and situation, e.g. talking and behaving appropriately at a job interview, or talking in a second language. When teachers come out of role, they can then talk with their pupils about the style and content of the language that was used.

How to set it up

If pupils are not yet used to working with their 'Teacher-in-Role', the teacher can always just try out the strategy with them for a minute or two initially, then come out of role and briefly talk with the pupils about the experience before going back into role for longer.

Pupils need to know all the time whether they are working in or out of role and whether their teacher is. Teachers should not suddenly go into role without any preparation or warning. They need to clearly sign the role for the class in some way, e.g. by wearing a simple piece of costume, or carrying some relevant object, to 'sign', or signify, when they are in role. For example, they might simply say, 'Whenever I am wearing this shawl, I will be in role, as the wise old woman. Whenever I take the shawl off, I will no longer be in role as her', or, 'Whenever I am carrying this lamp, I am Florence Nightingale . . .', etc. Teachers can just inform their pupils when they are going into role and when they have come out again, but signing the role by carrying an object, or by wearing a simple piece of costume, makes it visually clear – and is particularly helpful if the teacher is going to take on different roles at various points in the lesson.

Teachers should only stay in role for as long as is necessary for the role to achieve its purpose. They also need to come out of role if the role is not working well and achieving its purpose. Teachers can always try a different role, or even a different strategy altogether.

Teacher tips

- Know what you intend the main function and purpose of the role to be, in relation to the pupils' learning.
- Always make it clear to the pupils, when and whether you (and they) are in or out of role.
- Do not slide in and out of role unexpectedly, as this is confusing and hampers the make-believe.
- You do not need to be an 'actor' but you do need to sustain a role with seriousness, commitment, and purpose. Do not be in role half-heartedly or overact!
- Do not stay in role for longer than you need to. Come out of role once the role has achieved its purpose, or if it is not achieving what you want it to.
- Try taking on different status roles sometimes and resist the temptation to just adopt high-status roles for control purposes. When teachers take on roles that are of lower status than those of their pupils, it can be far more enabling for the pupils.

5.3 Meetings

What it offers

Meetings can happen within fictional contexts yet be dealing with realistic problems and issues of concern. They can proceed 'as if' they are real-life meetings and can have similar protocols. Pupils can learn about how to run and contribute to meetings and can practice and develop the associated skills. What they are learning about meetings, and the skills they practise during them, are likely to be of use in their future working lives, e.g. active listening, communication, turn-taking, assertiveness and diplomacy, focusing, informative and persuasive speech, etc.

The class can give and receive information in role at meetings. They can discuss issues and problems that a fictional community is having; share viewpoints, opinions, and ideas; and suggest (and maybe vote on) possible actions. The class can experience participation in meetings. Some may be functioning democratically, and others may not. They can experience meetings at which they are allowed to speak freely and others at which their contributions are being restricted or silenced. The meetings within fictional contexts might be formal or informal, secret or public, planned or spontaneous, and/or by invitation only or open to all.

Meetings might require pupils to write in role, in different ways during and/or after the meeting, for various purposes and a range of audiences, e.g. agendas, reports, informal note-taking, and formal minute-taking. Meetings provide opportunities for pupils to present thoughts, feelings, opinions, and viewpoints to each other, and to be listened to. Within a fictional context, a pupil may be voicing opinions and views that are not congruent with those they hold in real life, and they may need to explain and justify them. This may help them to better understand and tolerate viewpoints and opinions in real life that differ from their own. At meetings, they might sometimes be expected to cast their vote (either secretly or publicly), and this offers a practical way for them to can learn about voting processes. They might also learn that voting can sometimes be rigged!

Teachers in role can take part in meetings. They might chair the meeting, contribute to it, or just attend and observe without necessarily contributing. A 'Teacher-in-Role' (Section 5.2) at a meeting might sometimes be intentionally provocative and controversial in order to stimulate the pupils to respond more. They might align themselves with the weakest side during a discussion or debate to help balance the arguments heard at the meeting.

How to set it up

Meetings can be set up as informal discussions, or as more formal meetings with certain protocols, and a process to follow. For example, the pupils as the villagers of Hamelin might meet in the marketplace and talk together informally about the rat plague, or the teacher might get them together to semi-formally discuss the problem at a meeting. They could go to a formal council meeting and complain about the rats, to the mayor and the corporation.

At any meeting, the teacher can choose whether to have an active role themselves or not. They might decide to chair a meeting sometimes (and can use the opportunity to model how to chair meetings), or they might ask the pupils themselves to organise and run the meeting.

The teacher can attend in role and decide whether to remain silent or contribute during the meeting.

Meetings can sometimes be temporarily halted, reflectively discussed (out of role) for learning purposes, and then resumed.

Teacher tips

- Before the meeting starts, make sure the class know the meeting protocols. This can be done out of role by the teacher, just before a meeting starts. Alternatively, it can be done in role at the start of the meeting (by whoever is the chair).
- Before the meeting starts, you may wish to allocate some specific tasks to individual pupils (or groups of pupils), e.g. note-taking, introducing a speaker, meeting and greeting people on arrival and maybe accompanying VIPs to their seats, time-keeping, etc.

5.4 Mantle of the Expert

What it offers

'Mantle of the Expert' (Heathcote and Bolton, 1995; Taylor, 2016), gives pupils opportunities to work in role and complete tasks together 'as if' they are experts with specialist knowledge and skills. This can lead them towards enquiry-based learning, as they often need to gain more knowledge about a subject to complete their work-related tasks as 'experts'. They may be completing tasks as scientists, historians, archivists, journalists, social workers, museum curators, town planners, etc. The pupils will be using and applying real knowledge and skills when carrying out their tasks, albeit within a fictional context. The work they embark on is usually commissioned by an external client (often the 'Teacher-in-Role').

When pupils are working in role as experts, they feel that they have high status and start to treat each other 'as if' they are all professionals. They are working as a team and are collectively responsible and accountable to their clients. They will start to behave confidently in role, 'as if' they are professionals at work. They may start using unfamiliar vocabulary and talk in ways that fit with the imagined context and signal that they have the expertise.

The 'Teacher-in-Role' as the external client usually commissions the task, but the teacher might decide to take on other roles, too, as the work progresses, e.g. by becoming the experts' assistant or the client's intermediary.

Whilst working on the task as a team of experts, the pupils are using and developing actual work-related skills, e.g. they research and share ideas, discuss possibilities, and select and reject ideas together, and they create, refine, and present plans to each other and to the external client. They may be keeping their client informed of progress (sometimes through written reports) and are often working to a deadline.

How to set it up

The teacher knows the curriculum and needs to decide the learning focus. The teacher might first teach a traditional knowledge-based lesson or two that links to the subject matter, and then start to use 'Mantle of the Expert' so that the pupils are given the opportunity to use and apply their knowledge and become motivated to find out more.

The teacher decides what that imaginary context and commission are going to be. Then, in role as the client, the teacher meets with the experts (the class) and explains what is required of them. The tasks are usually linked nowadays to the school's planned curriculum, which may be subject-specific and/or cross-curricular (Table 5.1).

Table 5.1 'Mantle of the Expert' examples

The client	The experts	Some possible commissions and subsequent tasks
Theme park entrepreneur	Designers of theme parks	Design *'The Ultimate Theme Park'*. Research the competition online, then create and draw draft plans in groups. Groups present their draft plans to each other, then take some ideas from each plan and collaboratively create the plan that will be presented to external client. Meet with and update the entrepreneur (or their representative) from time to time.
Museum director	Museum curators	*Curate a museum exhibition*, linked to a history topic, e.g. Victorian Children, World War II Evacuees, Ancient Egyptians, Ancient Greeks, the Vikings, etc. Search for relevant historical artefacts online. Select a limited number of artefacts to exhibit, then print off and label the images. Discuss and agree how to best display the artefacts. Produce an exhibition design plan and present it to the museum director. Write about each artefact, for the exhibition catalogue. Create an advert for the exhibition. Assemble and then publicly present the exhibition. Email and meet with the museum director from time to time, to give an update on progress.
Art gallery director	Curators of art exhibitions	*Curate an Art Exhibition*. Search for and select pictures for an art exhibition about an art movement, theme, or named artist, e.g. Impressionism, heroes and leaders, Georgia O'Keefe. Search for relevant pieces of art online. Select a limited number to exhibit, then print off and label the images. Discuss and agree how to best display the art. Produce an art exhibition design plan and present it to the gallery director. Write about each piece of art for the exhibition catalogue. Assemble and then publicly present the display. Email and meet with the art gallery director from time to time, in order to give an update on progress.
The king	Wolf hunters	Design a trap to catch the last living wolf (unharmed) and design the perfect environment for keeping the wolf in captivity. Based on the picture book *The Last Wolf* (Turnbull, 1995)

Teacher tips

- Stay alert to what the pupils are saying when they are being 'experts', as it might offer some unexpected learning opportunities that lead into additional, worthwhile tasks.
- Dorothy Heathcote (the founder of 'Mantle of the Expert') herself deliberately avoided using the term 'expert' with the pupils.

5.5 Eavesdropping

What it offers

There are times in lessons when pairs or groups of pupils are talking with each other simultaneously. They may be seated in fixed groups or moving around the room, freely talking with each other. 'Eavesdropping' can be used in any subject lesson to let everyone overhear bits of each other's conversations in turn. When it is their turn to be overheard, the pairs or groups can either go back and repeat something that they have already said, 'as if' saying it for the first time, or they might decide to just continue their conversation, with the rest of the class listening. If they choose to go back and repeat something that they have already said, then they might, in the retelling, slightly refine what was originally said. If pupils know in advance that they are going to be listened to in this way afterwards (even for a short time), they may be more likely to stay 'on task'.

In drama lessons, the conversations are usually happening in role, within a dramatic context. The strategy is sometimes referred to during drama and theatre making as 'overheard conversations' (Neelands and Goode, 1990, page 29).

How to set it up

When conversations are underway, the teacher calls out, 'Freeze!' (see 'Freeze-frame', Section 5.11), then explains that they will now move around the room and 'eavesdrop' on what is being said. Everyone then remains still and silent, until the teacher is standing nearest to them. It will then be their turn to be overheard, until the teacher moves away and goes to the next pair or group instead. Once the teacher moves away, the overheard group will freeze again. Pupils may need reminding that when it is their turn to be overheard, they do need to speak loud enough for everyone to hear, i.e. project their voices.

Teacher tips

- The teacher can signal that they are 'eavesdropping' by cupping their hand around their ear, whilst standing by each group and listening.
- Pupils can be asked to imagine that their teacher is functioning as a loudspeaker. When the teacher is standing near to them, their voices need to be amplified, so that they can be easily heard by everyone.
- If pupils are not speaking loud enough to be heard by everyone, then when it is their turn, the teacher can mime turning a large, imaginary volume knob to signal that they need to speak louder.
- Younger children can be introduced to 'performance dust'. The teacher sprinkles some on themselves first, to demonstrate that it makes voices louder. Performance dust can be sprinkled over everyone before the 'eavesdropping' starts. Sprinkling performance dust over a head can also be used as a signal by the teacher during any performance if there are voices that need to be louder.

5.6 Eyewitness

What it offers

Pupils can be asked to carefully observe a scene, 'as if' they are invisible eyewitnesses watching it. The scene they are looking at might be happening live or could be a recorded scene. It might just be a static scene, captured in a photograph, painting, or 'still image' (Section 5.12). Being told they are eyewitnesses at the scene can lead to pupils paying greater attention to what they are looking at. They can talk about the scene at the time and/or afterwards and in different ways, e.g. informatively or descriptively. They can recount what they saw to pupils who were not eyewitnesses with them at the scene. They can be asked to look at the same scene or image, but from different viewpoints (literally and/or metaphorically), and this can sometimes lead to them interpreting the same scene differently. They might be asked to look at the same scene but with a narrow, restricted view, e.g. through their fingers or through a tube. They then need to listen to each other to try and piece together what they all saw.

Scenes and images that have been 'eyewitnessed' can provide the stimulus and content for subsequent writing, e.g. eyewitness recounts and statements, diary entries and letters, newspaper reports (if the scene was newsworthy), and first- or third-person narratives.

How to set it up

The pupils are invited to become invisible eyewitnesses at a scene. It could be an improvised scene, one that a group has devised, or a scene depicted in a 'still image' of some sort that is projected on the wall or screen. They then enter and position themselves near or around the scene, 'as if' they are eyewitnesses. The teacher needs to make it clear that they are not expected to get interactively involved in the scene. The teacher might forewarn them that they could be answering questions about the scene afterwards, so it is important that they observe the scene carefully.

In drama lessons, the scenes are usually performed live by a group of students. However, teachers of other subjects may wish to project film footage, photographs, or historic paintings of real-life scenes, e.g. climate change protestors, a rescue, a natural disaster, a tribe, an accident, a refugee camp.

Linked activities and variations

- The eyewitnesses can enter in pairs and talk to each other 'in the moment' whilst observing the scene 'in the moment'. They can talk again together after the scene, and talk with other pairs of eyewitnesses.
- Having all witnessed the scene, they can then get into pairs. One of them will pretend that they did not witness the scene and asks their partner about it. Then they swap, so both get a chance to give a verbal recount and both get the opportunity to ask questions. If the scene was a newsworthy one, then one of the pair could be in role as a newspaper reporter.
- It can be set up so that only half the pupils are eyewitnesses who talk afterwards with those who were not at the scene, describing it to them and answering their questions.

The scene can then be shown again and the original eyewitnesses can receive feedback from their peers about how accurately they described the scene.
- The teacher can become one of the eyewitnesses and/or could take on the role of a newspaper reporter afterwards, interviewing the pupils as eyewitnesses (see 'Teacher-in-Role', Section 5.2).
- Who might need to know about the scene? This question could lead to the teacher taking a role, that enables the pupils to recount the scene and answer questions about it as eye-witnesses. For example, if the scene was of an accident, then the teacher might become a police officer and the eyewitnesses might need to write and sign witness statements.

5.7 Rumours

What it offers

Everyone gets the opportunity in role to make up, spread, and embellish rumours, which are usually about a fictional character, event, or situation with which they have just engaged in some way. The rumours could, for example, be about a scene which the pupils have just participated in or watched, or a character they have just spoken with, e.g. the 'Teacher-in-Role'. Rumouring usually generates many ideas and narrative possibilities quickly, with the class working collaboratively, listening attentively, thinking creatively, and responding spontaneously. The pupils may be creating new rumours and/or changing and elaborating on those they have heard.

This strategy can be adapted and used instead, for spreading factual information about a subject, e.g. in a History lesson, the class could be asked to move around the room, telling each other what they know (and may have researched themselves) about a given historical character or event. They can gather and spread information and maybe add to it something relevant and true. Afterwards, the information can be gathered, considered, and some 'facts' may then need to be verified by the pupils.

How to set it up

This strategy is useful when something has occurred within a narrative, that would probably result in gossip and rumour, e.g. Duncan the king has been murdered. The teacher can invite the students to spread gossip and rumour about this, maybe in role as servants. The spreading of rumours starts and stops with a signal from the teacher. The teacher might lead into the 'Rumours' activity by briefly storytelling what has led to the rumours and gossip (see 'Teacher as Storyteller', Section 5.8), e.g. 'When the servants in the castle heard of Duncan's murder, the rumours started to spread . . .' (then 'Rumours' starts).

The teacher can join in 'Rumours', too, to add authentic information and make comments that might provoke deeper thinking, e.g. 'Macbeth *said* that he killed the guards, but that seems odd to me' or 'They say that Lady Macbeth was so shocked that she fainted, but I think she was just pretending to faint'.

The 'Teacher-in-Role' (Section 5.2) as an equal can gather everyone around after a while and in role provoke a gossipy discussion, about the various rumours that are flying around.

Teacher tips

- Tell the class that the most effective rumours are believable, and the challenge is to make their rumours sound believable.
- If pupils stay talking with the same people too long, then the rumours do not spread, so you can call out 'Move on!' or 'Change!' Everyone then moves on to share rumours with and gather rumours from others.
- If there are plenty of rumours spreading, then do not let the activity go on for too long, (two or three minutes is usually long enough). You do not need dozens of rumours, and they can become more farcical after a while.

Linked activities and variations

- Each student selects one sentence or phrase from a rumour that they initiated or helped spread. The class then gather with their eyes closed, select a sentence or phrase from a rumour and voice it during a 'Voice Collage' (Section 5.32).
- The various rumours about a character can be written on separate self-adhesive labels and placed around a 'Role on the Wall' (Section 5.29). The more likely the rumour is to be true, the closer it can be positioned in relation to the character's outline.
- Some of the rumours may be true, whereas others will be plausible or unlikely. On a large floor space, the teacher can indicate where an imaginary 'probability line' starts and finishes. One end of the line represents 'false' and the other end 'true'. In turn, each pupil can step forward, speak any rumour and position themselves on the line wherever they think is most appropriate for that rumour (see 'Spectrum of Difference/Spectrogram', Section 5.26).
- When the rumours are about a character, the class can stand in a circle around that character (or around an object that represents the character). In turn, each pupil can be given the opportunity to cross the circle and speak a rumour about the character (or to the character) as they pass by him or her (see 'Passing Thoughts', Section 5.24).

5.8 Teacher as Storyteller

What it offers

Storytelling is a type of performance and some teachers are very good at it. Teachers as good storytellers can model various ways of talking and can choose what to focus the pupil's attention on as they tell the story. They need to tune in with the responses of their audience and might play with their audience sometimes. Teachers as storytellers will pause at certain moments to give them emphasis and to allow sufficient time for their pupils to process what they are hearing and seeing. The pupils are not just listening; they will also be watching and interpreting the storyteller's gestures, movements, and expressions in conjunction with what the storyteller is saying. As a storyteller, the teacher can build up dramatic tension towards significant moments. Storytelling also is an opportunity for teachers to present and use unfamiliar vocabulary within a meaningful context and use vocabulary that the pupils are familiar with – appropriately, effectively, and contextually. Listening and watching their teachers perform as storytellers can have a positive impact on the pupils as storytellers themselves, and on subsequent story writing. Good storytelling by teachers gains and sustains pupils' attention, deepens their emotional and cognitive engagement with the story, and helps make the story more meaningful and memorable.

The stories that a teacher tells can be true or fictitious. Historical stories can come alive when told dramatically. The teacher can tell the same story, but in either the first or third person, e.g. 'as if' they are a villager who has survived the plague in Eyam, or just telling the story of the villagers of Eyam, as a third person narrative. There are some storytelling strategies that get the class actively involved in the storytelling too, alongside the 'Teacher as Storyteller' (see 'Active Storytelling', Section 5.9 and 'Whoosh!', Section 5.10).

The story that a teacher dramatically recounts could be one that the class has created together, perhaps through 'Small Group Playmaking' (Section 5.15) or by creating and sequencing 'still images' (Section 5.12). The pupil's scenes or images can be represented silently, with an accompanying and continuous narrative being provided by the 'Teacher as Storyteller'. When the pupils hear their own scenes being recounted by the 'Teacher as Storyteller', it elevates and gives status to their story-making and can be helpful to the pupils, who are developing their own skills as storytellers and as story writers.

How to set it up

Storytelling is a type of theatre performance and the pupils are the audience. The class needs to be comfortable (probably seated) and be able to see and hear the teacher clearly. The teacher needs to ensure that they have the full attention of the class before they start telling the story. As happens in the theatre (once the curtain has opened), the class may be held waiting in silent anticipation for a few seconds before the storytelling starts.

Teacher tips

- Engage with and be responsive to the class as your audience. You need to keep their attention throughout.

- Speak clearly and effectively and try to communicate meaning and not just linear content.
- Do not just 'tell' the story. Use gesture and movement meaningfully, and use your voice expressively, too. Stir and play on their emotions (making the story more engaging and memorable).
- Be clear, concise, and engaging as a storyteller and avoid losing their attention by rambling unnecessarily.

Linked activities and variations

- The groups each sit in a space. The teacher tells the story and approaches each group when it is their turn to briefly perform their mime, 'still image', or scene that depicts that moment in the story. Once a group has finished performing, the teacher seamlessly continues storytelling and travels on to the next group in the sequence. The whole experience can be set up 'as if' it is a collaborative performance, with a theatrical atmosphere maintained throughout (as in 'Small Group Playmaking', Section 5.15).
- The class sits in a large circle. The performance space is within the circle (theatre in the round). The teacher tells the story and the groups enter and perform their 'still image', mime, or short scene when it is their turn at the appropriate moment in the storytelling. They should be asked to enter the space 'in the manner of actors', perform, then return to the edge of the circle. The teacher continues as the storyteller, with other groups entering and performing in turn, until the story is ended.
- A 'Teacher as Storyteller' might choose to tell only the opening and end of the story. As a storyteller, they can set the scene and create the atmosphere, then remain silent as the groups in turn perform their series of mimes, short scenes, or illustrative 'still images' (see 'Small Group Playmaking', Section 5.15 and 'Still Images', Section 5.12). The 'Teacher as Storyteller' can then conclude the story, bringing it meaningfully to a close once the last group have performed.
- One person in each group can become a storyteller who narrates what is happening in their group's scene. The teacher can still be the first and last storyteller, opening and closing the story, with pupils storytelling in between.

5.9 Active Storytelling

What it offers

The simplest form of 'Active Storytelling' involves everyone in the class individually and simultaneously miming a story, whilst it is being told by the teacher. The teacher mimes the story as they are telling it to the pupils and they imitate and mimic the teacher's actions, gestures, and expressions. Alternatively, they might be given the opportunity to spontaneously create their own appropriate actions, etc., as the story is told. Embodying a story through mime is fun and helps make the story more memorable.

'Active Storytelling' is an inclusive way of introducing an unfamiliar story to a class but can also be used as a way of literally 're-membering' a story that the class already knows. Everyone in the class is bringing the characters and scenes to life. Pupils tend to become so focused on their own mimes that they are not really watching each other's, and this can be helpful for any pupils who might feel inhibited when they are miming for an audience.

'Active Storytelling' can be used with any story, whether true or fictional. Historic moments and events can be re-enacted and remembered in this way, e.g. escaping from the Great Fire of London, or the sinking of the Titanic. In English, narrative poems can be approached through 'Active Storytelling'. Also, when class novels are being read, 'Active Storytelling' can be used as a way of helping the class remember what has happened so far, before going on to read the next chapter. In drama lessons, if pupils have created a story together, then 'Active Storytelling' can be used at the end of the lesson, as a way of enabling the class to recount and remember their story.

How to set it up

Everyone stands in a space and faces the teacher. The teacher tells and mimes the story, in an expressive way. The pupils join in, individually miming whatever is happening in the story at that moment. The teacher can emphasise key moments and episodes in the story by miming them for longer. This can help make significant parts of the story more memorable.

The mimes during 'Active Storytelling' are usually carried out individually and the class may be asked to mime silently, so that the storytelling can always be clearly heard.

Teacher tips

- 'Active Storytelling' can be done with the class and teacher standing together in a circle. This enables the class to see the storyteller and see each other miming. It may help if you start with the pupils spaced out around the room and once they become more familiar with 'Active Storytelling', then move on to using a circle formation. This stepped approach can be helpful for any pupils who might initially feel self-conscious about being watched as they mime.
- Pupils usually find it easier to focus on the storyteller and the story, if they are facing the storyteller and can see them as well as hear them.

Linked activities and variations

- Pupils can mime the story first (with the teacher telling the story), then move on to actively recounting the story to themselves and/or to a partner.
- Miming and recounting a story first can be helpful to pupils who are going to subsequently write the story.

5.10 Whoosh!

What it offers

This is a form of 'Active Storytelling' that is often used to familiarise pupils with the characters, settings, plots, and subplots of a text, e.g. a play by Shakespeare, before they go on to read and explore it in greater depth. It can also be used with stories with which students are already familiar, to get them literally 're-membering' the story.

The class teacher is usually the storyteller, so can decide which moments in the narrative warrant the greatest emphasis. A 'Whoosh!' is inclusive. Everyone is standing together in a circle and gets several turns at stepping into the circle and miming whatever is happening in the story, at that moment. Whilst storytelling, the teacher works their way along the class circle, signalling when the next pupil (or group of pupils) need to step forward and mime. The teacher decides how many pupils will step forward and mime each time and can subtly enable or avoid giving solo mime opportunities to specific pupils. As the whole class is not usually miming simultaneously during a 'Whoosh!', those performing the mime have an audience of peers who will also be performing when their turn comes. Storytelling with a 'Whoosh!' is quite speedy, so nobody needs to mime for long.

How to set it up

The class stands in a circle. The centre is the stage area. The teacher explains that they will be telling the class a story. As the story proceeds, the storyteller (usually the teacher) moves along the circle, sequentially signalling in turn to students (and groups of students) to step forward and mime whatever is going on in the story at that moment. They might become people or significant objects in the scene, for example. The teacher needs to decide and tell the pupils whether they are expected to mime silently or whether they can make sounds and speak.

As the story progresses and the storyteller moves along the circle, they will signal when (and how many) pupils should step forward at the different points in the story to take their turn. The acting area within the circle will gradually become crowded and need to be cleared, so from time to time, the storyteller will simply call out 'Whoosh! Whoosh! Whoosh!' repeatedly, whilst waving their arms from side to side. This is the signal for everyone to move back to the edge of the circle again. Once the space is clear, the storytelling and miming can continue until the story ends. The space will usually need to be cleared several times with a 'Whoosh!' before the story is over.

Teacher tips

- Teachers can give pupils the opportunity to signal 'pass' and not take their turn. However, they should remain in the class circle rather than sit out and watch. They might then decide to take their next turn.
- If the teacher knows that a student is shy and/or reluctant to step forward and perform, then it makes sense to include that student in a group mime rather than signalling for them to step forward and mime solo.

5.11 Freeze-frame

What it offers

A 'Freeze-frame' is arrived at by pausing a scene that is underway. The teacher can choose when, why, and how often to freeze a scene – and can always let the scene resume and perhaps freeze it again at some other point. When a scene is frozen, it gives a 'still image' that can be studied carefully, sometimes (literally) from different viewpoints. The class can be invited to study and comment on the stilled scene, either speaking freely or maybe using statement prompts such as 'I notice . . .', 'I think . . .', and 'I wonder . . .'.

Facial expressions, body language, and the relative distance and physical positioning of those in the scene can be looked at and thought about critically and collaboratively, whilst the scene stays frozen 'in the moment' (see 'Still Images', Section 5.12).

How to set it up

A 'Freeze-frame' is a 'still image' that has been arrived at suddenly and has not been devised. In a drama lesson, the class might be working in role when the teacher suddenly calls out 'Freeze!' Everyone stops instantly and holds their position very still. It can be likened to pressing a pause button.

It is not technically correct to ask students to *make* or *devise* a Freeze-frame, as there is no 'making' or 'devising' process involved. Pupils just need to obey the instruction 'Freeze!' and then hold their positions very still until instructed to do otherwise.

When the pupils have held their Freeze-frame still for quite a while, they might then be asked to melt the Freeze-frame in slow motion or to resume the action, i.e. as if the 'play' button has now been pressed.

Any teacher can purposefully call out 'Freeze!' in any lesson. It might simply be used when the teacher wants the full attention of the class immediately for some reason. Having acquired everyone's attention, it might be that the teacher will then go on to give or gather information, perhaps using a different strategy.

Teacher tips

- It is worth demonstrating how still you want the pupils to be and giving them some practice at freezing (to make your expectations clear). Do not accept still-ish! You can ask them to walk around the room. Whenever you call out 'Freeze!', they must immediately freeze their position and stay very still until you call out 'Move on', and then after a while 'Freeze' again, and so on.
- Freezing movement can also be practiced with music, e.g. 'Move when the music is playing. Freeze whenever the music stops'.
- Play some games that require them to freeze their movement, e.g. 'What's the time, Mr Wolf?', i.e. freezing whenever the wolf turns to tell them the time and running away when the wolf calls out 'Dinner time!'

- Remember that some pupils will find it harder than others to keep very still, e.g. very young children and/or those with attention deficit hyperactivity disorder (ADHD). Everyone just needs to keep as still as they can.
- Pupils will sometimes freeze in a position that is difficult to hold, e.g. standing on one leg. Let them know that they should reposition themselves, for comfort and safety, not wobble and risk falling.
- It can be helpful to use comparisons, e.g. 'Be as still as a photograph' or 'Stay as still as a picture in a picture book'.
- The teacher can demonstrate how still and silent they need to be, so that the class can see that there is a qualitative difference between being still and just 'still-ish'.

Some possible 'follow-on' strategies and next steps

- When pupils are in a 'Freeze-frame', they can be invited in turn to speak their inner thoughts at that moment, (see 'Thought-tracking', Section 5.18).
- Individuals can be invited to thaw for a while to answer questions before freezing back into position again (see 'Hot-seating', Section 5.17).

5.12 Still Images

What it offers

Images that have been thoughtfully constructed can communicate much to those who study them. The process of devising and constructing images in an embodied way is often a memorable and helpful learning experience in itself for those involved. Images can be spontaneously created, carefully devised, or replicated, using the body (or bodies). When physically replicating an existing image such as a painting or statue, pupils first need to study the image carefully to be able to replicate it. Alternatively, if the images are not replicas but are an embodiment of their own ideas, then they will be using some other skills during the devising process. They will be inter-thinking creatively and critically, and discussing and agreeing what to include in their 'still image' and how to do so effectively and meaningfully, collectively and with only their static bodies. If an audience of their peers will be looking at their 'still image', then they may also need to consider where their audience will be positioned. Their audience is usually static, but teachers might sometimes invite the audience to move around and study a group's 'still image' from various angles and viewpoints.

Some possible curriculum links

Pupils are often asked to study various images, particularly in arts and humanities lessons. Photographs, picture books and illustrations, paintings, statues, sculptures, carvings, stained-glass windows, graphic novels, tapestries, and posters are all examples of 'still images' that pupils might focus on in various subject lessons. For example, they can study, then be asked to physically replicate parts of The Bayeux Tapestry (1070) or a painting of The Great Fire of London Battlehooke, J. (1675) or The Death of Nelson Maclise, D. (1864). They can replicate and embody existing portraits and statues, or physically become new statues for historical and/or fictional characters. They can physically become an illustration, for any type of text, e.g. the narrative poem The Highwayman by Alfred Noyes (1906) or a stained-glass window depicting a scene from the Bible (a sacred text), or become an additional image for seamless inclusion in an existing picture book or graphic novel such as The Arrival (Tan, 2006). They can physically become the images to illustrate myths and legends, fairy tales and traditional stories, nursery rhymes, etc.

'Still images' can be replicas of photographs that the pupils are studying. They may have been taken at significant moments, e.g. recent photographs of refugees afloat at sea in overcrowded boats, or climate change protestors, or children being evacuated from London by train during the World War II. Some photographs are intentionally posed for, and 'still images' can be devised and presented 'as if' they are such photographs, e.g. a wedding photograph or a staged photograph taken by a press photographer.

Texts read in English lessons often contain visual imagery which pupils can locate, select from, and make memorable through embodiment, using the 'still images' strategy. Their 'still images' based on texts can be presented afterwards, maybe with the accompanying text also being spoken.

Photographs and illustrations are sometimes used as starting points for PSHE and Relationships Education. The teacher might ask the students to make a 'still image' of a realistic, fictional problem in a school playground. When doing this, they will inevitably be drawing on their personal knowledge of playground moments, but the 'still image' is of a fictitious playground, therefore providing a safely distanced starting point for discussing, exploring, and maybe resolving conflict.

As in art, 'still images' do not always need to be realistic. They can sometimes be abstract, symbolic, or surreal (for example, a 'still image' can be based on themes, concepts, ideas, emotions, memories, hopes, and anxieties). A teacher might (for example) ask pupils to devise a 'still image' with the title *Hope* or *Nightmare*.

How to set it up

The pupils can be asked to replicate, devise, create, or make 'still images' using just their bodies. They can be asked to make themselves into a specific type of 'still image', such as a painting, statue, photograph, etc. They might be asked to make their 'still images' in pairs or small groups, in which case they will need some time to share their ideas with each other, select and try out ideas, maybe refine their images, and rehearse presenting them. If they are going to share their 'still images' with each other afterwards, it is best to let them know this at the outset, so that they can consider where their audience will be viewing it from.

There are many warm-up activities that can be used to get pupils focused on using their bodies to make images.

Linked activities and variations

- The class walks around the room. Whenever the teacher calls out a word or phrase, everyone stops walking and forms an individual 'still image', physically depicting the given word or phrase, e.g. 'peace' or 'drowning' or 'Is this a dagger which I see before me?' (*Macbeth*).
- The class walks around the room. Whenever the teacher calls out a word or phrase, everyone partners with the nearest person, and silently, the pairs quickly form a 'still image' together, depicting the given word or phrase, e.g. 'Power' or 'Leaving home'.
- In groups, one pupil becomes the director and gives verbal directions to the other group members until the 'still image' is complete. The director can be instructed to keep their hands behind their backs, and not model with their own bodies what they want the group to do with theirs.

Assembling and dissembling 'still images'

'Still images' can be collaboratively and silently constructed by groups or whole classes, with students entering the space in turn, adding themselves silently to build a tableau, (a replicated or original image), e.g. a crowded boat of refugees.

Rather than suddenly break up the tableau afterwards, it can be slowly dissembled, with one student at a time withdrawing slowly and silently from it. This can be done in reverse order, i.e. the last person who entered the 'still image' leaves it first. Alternatively, the order could be random or 'first in, last out' (although the latter can be more physically problematic).

Entering and extending projected images

- Project a painting or photograph onto a large wall. Each student enters in turn and positions themself as someone who they can see in the picture (maybe leading into 'Improvisation', Section 5.1).
- Project a picture or photograph onto the large wall. In turn, the students each enter and position themselves as an object they can see in the picture (maybe leading into 'Talking Objects', Section 5.42).
- Project a picture or photograph onto the wall. In turn, the students enter and position themselves 'as if' they are a feature of the man-made and/or natural landscape setting that can be seen (maybe leading into 'Talking Objects', Section 5.42).
- The students in turn enter a painting or photograph that is being projected on a large wall. They become additional characters in the scene who are eyewitnesses to it. They may be invisible eyewitnesses, but in a crowd scene they can just add themselves to the crowd. Thinking to themselves as an eyewitness (or talking with other eyewitnesses, either 'in the moment' or later) can be helpful if pupils are going to be writing eyewitness recounts afterwards. They can also answer questions later as eyewitnesses (see 'Hot-seating', Section 5.17).
- A single image can be projected onto a wall, e.g. from a picture book, a painting, or a photograph. The pupils can then be invited to enter in turn and extend the given image by adding themselves to main image and/or extending it by adding themselves to the left and/or right of the given image. As each pupil gets into position, they say aloud what (or who) they are and add just a little more information, e.g. 'I am a wooden bench and people often sit on me and talk'.
- When being shown any image, the class can be told that they are highly skilled 'picture detectives'. The teacher can tell them that most people just notice the obvious things in a picture but because they are 'picture detectives', they will notice things that most people do not. They can then be invited to say what they have noticed, just using the sentence stem, 'I notice . . .', e.g. 'I notice that the victim is not looking at the bully' or, 'I notice that this boat only has men and children on it'. After a while, the teacher might change the sentence stem to, 'I wonder', e.g. 'I wonder if anyone will help the victim' or 'I wonder where the children's mothers are'.

Contrasting 'still images'

- Individually, in pairs or groups, pupils can be asked to use their bodies to present a pair of contrasting 'still images', e.g. 'I want you to make your bodies into two statues. The title of the first statue is *The Ideal* and the title of the second is *The Reality*' (Boal, 2019). They then move in slow motion and silence, to become the first statue. They freeze as the first statue for a few seconds (see 'Freeze-frame', Section 5.11), then transition in slow motion, to form the second statue.
- The pupils are in pairs. The teacher calls out a pair of contrasting words, e.g. 'war and peace' or 'hopeful and hopeless'. Silently and in slow motion (with no prior discussion),

they slowly move into one 'still image' together that portrays both words. They can then be asked to slowly and silently transition, swapping their relative positions.
- The pupils are in groups. Each group devises and presents a 'still image' of the same subject matter but in a different way, maybe from alternative viewpoints or at different points in time.

5.13 Sculpting

What it offers

'Sculpting' is a way of enabling a 'still image' to be gradually moulded and created by one pupil, using their partner 'as if' they are just a malleable lump of compliant clay. The pupil who is the clay bends to the sculptor's touch. The sculptor is in control and physically moulds their partner into a statue. Alternatively, the sculptor can be asked to only give verbal instructions and directions to the clay and not use any physical touch. They might even be asked to keep their hands behind their backs, so that can only use language to get the statue they want. Also, the pupil who is the lump of clay can be asked to keep their eyes closed so that they can only respond to what they are being told to do verbally and cannot pick up on the sculptor's gestures and expressions.

How to set it up

This activity is usually carried out in pairs, with one pupil being a lump of clay and the other being the sculptor. The sculptor uses touch to mould their compliant partner into a sculpture (a still image). Afterwards, they usually swap so that both pupils get a turn at being the sculptor and the clay.

The teacher might inform the pupils what the title of the sculpture is and then ask the sculptors to mould it accordingly ('as if' they are working to a commission), e.g. the title could be *Victory*, *The Leader*, *Hope*, *We Will Never Forget*, etc. Alternatively, the teacher might let the sculptor decide the title afterwards.

Linked activities and variations

- Everyone starts off on the ground as individual lumps of clay. In slow motion, each pupil moves and gradually forms themselves into a statue, and then freezes into position (see 'Freeze-frame', Section 5.11). The pupils can be asked to then reverse the process gradually, and in slow motion revert to becoming the lump of clay again. The clay can keep reforming itself and becoming a different statue each time.
- When half the pupils are staying very still 'as if' they are sculptures, the sculptors then can be asked to move around the room 'as if' they are all in a sculpture park together. This gives all the sculptors the opportunity to have look at each other's sculptures and maybe talk together about them in role (see 'Improvisation', Section 5.1) as they move around the statue park.
- Sculptures can be asked to speak their titles aloud to any passers-by, or alternatively, the sculptor might have written the title of the sculpture onto a sentence strip and places it by their statue.

5.14 3D Storyboard

What it offers

A 'Storyboard' is a series of 'still image' that are presented chronologically and tell a story through just a sequence of pictures (rather like comics and graphic novels do). Storyboards are usually drawn but pupils can be asked to use their bodies to form a series of images that tell a story. They can then present the images physically and sequentially in turn, resulting in a '3D Storyboard'. Alternatively, groups of pupils can each be given a different episode from the same story to embody as a 'still images'. When each group in turn presents their image, as one in a chronological sequence of images, then this results in a collective '3D Storyboard' (see 'Performance Carousel', Section 5.16).

Some possible curriculum links

Triptychs consist of three paintings that are usually presented on three adjacent panels. Early triptychs often depicted stories from the Bible (with a central panel and 'wings'). The three panels together often present a narrative chronologically, e.g. *The Pioneer* by the Australian artist Frederick McCubbin (1904). However, other artists have less conventionally used the three images of a triptych to offer different perspectives, thoughts, or feelings rather than depict a linear narrative, e.g. Francis Bacon's *Three Studies for Figures at the Base of a Crucifixion* (1944).

Triptychs can be embodied to become a '3D Storyboard' and 'missing' images can be created and added to it. The pupils' additional images can be photographed and perhaps added electronically to the original series of images, or maybe even painted 'in the style of the artist' and subsequently added. Technically speaking, it would then become a 'polyptych', i.e. a piece of art consisting of four or more panels.

Pupils can be asked to present a chronological series of images that depict a true story, such as an historical event. A '3D Storyboard' can be performed silently or accompanied by a verbal recount that narrates what is happening within each image in turn. Giving a narrative recount alongside a '3D Storyboard' can be particularly helpful if pupils are then going on to write the story.

A story, narrative poem, or play that a class has read in English lessons can have its key moments and scenes literally 're-membered' and then presented chronologically and physically as a '3D Storyboard' (with or without an accompanying narrative recount).

In PSHE and relationships lessons, an incomplete series of 'still images' can be devised and presented as a '3D Storyboard', e.g. the 'last' image might show the moment a child is about to steal a toy, the moment a playground bully starts confronting a victim, etc. When the 'last' given image is of a pivotal moment, the pupils can be asked to consider what the next image might depict. Various possible 'next' images can be suggested, discussed, devised, and presented by different groups.

Possible 'next images' can also be arrived at through 'Improvisation' (Section 5.1), with groups bringing the 'last' given 'still image' to life for a short time. The improvised scene can be frozen, resulting in a 'Freeze-frame' (Section 5.11) which might then be accepted as the next image in the '3D Storyboard'. However, any image can be brought alive more than once and improvised differently, leading to different (maybe more positive) outcomes from which to select.

How to set it up

Ask the students to use their bodies to form a series of 'still images' that depict the main episodes of a story in chronological order. They will need to discuss and agree what to show in each image and practise moving into and out of the sequence of images. It is best to ask groups to move between each of the images seamlessly and in slow motion, rather than just abruptly changing between each of their images (see 'Performance Carousel', Section 5.16).

Teacher tips

- The more images they are asked to devise and present, the more challenging the overall task will become. Creating and transitioning between three images is usually sufficient for any one group. However, you can give different parts of a story to different groups, with each group performing between one or three images in turn. Cumulatively and collaboratively, the class then ends up telling the whole story.

Some possible 'follow-on' strategies and next steps

- Each image is usually presented in silence, unless the teacher decides to give additional instructions, e.g. asking the groups to speak one sentence or thought 'in role' as the character they are portraying within the image (see 'Thought-tracking', Section 5.18). This is rather like listening to what might just appear visually within a speech bubble or thought bubble when reading a comic or graphic novel. Alternatively, the groups can be asked to voice an accompanying caption for each image.
- Make a large thought bubble and a large speech bubble from cardboard. When the teacher holds a speech or thought bubble close to any character within a 'still image' (Section 5.12), the pupil portraying that character is being invited to speak an 'in role' utterance or thought aloud (see 'Thought-tracking', Section 5.18).
- Characters can be invited to step out of a still image for a while and talk in role to themselves, directly to the audience, or to questioners (see 'Hot-seating', Section 5.17). Alternatively, they can remain within the image and talk in any of these ways.

5.15 Small Group Playmaking

What it offers

The skills being used and developed during 'Small Group Playmaking' are amongst those much valued in many workplaces, e.g. working together effectively as a team, creating something relevant to present collaboratively, and facing a deadline.

When a group of students devise and then perform a short scene to their peers, they first need to consider, understand, and agree what they are together trying to communicate to others, and why. Group scenes are usually short (often no longer that a minute or two), yet still require group members to think and talk creatively and critically together; to generate, share, discuss, and select ideas; and then find ways of communicating them meaningfully to others through a presentation or performance. During the 'play-making' process, pupils are using and developing a range of thinking skills, whilst refining and improving their scenes during rehearsal. They need to stay aware of their physical positioning, both in relation to each other and their real or imagined audience, and when speaking in scenes, they are getting the opportunity to practise projecting their voices well enough to be heard by everyone.

Groups will end up with different scenes, even when they are following the same set of instructions and working with the same stimulus. When groups watch each other's scenes, if they have been engaged in the same 'small Group Playmaking' task themselves, then they are in a unique position and have an immediate, strong connection and understanding of what they are watching.

Sequencing scenes

Groups can be asked to each create a short scene, depicting different moments or episodes from the same story (historical or fictional). The scenes can then be performed in chronological order (see 'Performance Carousel', Section 5.16).

Scenes can also be presented sequentially to present issues and situations of current concern and decline, that require action now, to prevent them from becoming worse, e.g. global warming, pollution, bullying.

'Split screen' scenes

Groups can each be asked to devise short scenes that are happening simultaneously in different settings, e.g. scenes inside different people's homes immediately after Prime Minister Neville Chamberlain announced on the wireless that Britain was at war (11.15 am, Sunday 3 September 1939), or the moment that a natural disaster happened, such as an earthquake, flood, or volcanic eruption. Group scenes can be performed simultaneously and then one at a time (or vice versa), using a 'Performance Carousel' (Section 5.16).

Teacher tips

- Let the groups know how long they have available for devising and rehearsing their scene and give them a countdown from time to time. They are unlikely to all be ready simultaneously, but stick to your deadline – even if a few individuals or a group say they are not ready to perform. Groups that are not ready can always be given the option of 'passing' and not performing on this occasion, or of performing their scene anyway, with those watching being made aware that it is 'work in progress' that is being shared.

Some possible 'follow-on' strategies and next steps

- After a group has performed a scene, the characters within the scene can be asked questions by those who have been watching it, i.e. the rest of the class. The character can physically remain in the scene whilst answering their questions in role, or can be invited to step out of the scene for a while and answer the questions (see 'Hot-seating', Section 5.17).

5.16 Performance Carousel

What it offers

This is a simple and effective way of enabling groups to seamlessly present in turn a series of 'still images' and/or a series of group performances without the need for a whole class rehearsal.

When groups are presenting their 'still images' or performing their short scenes in turn (see 'Small Group Playmaking', Section 5.15), it is important that the performing group has throughout the full attention of the other groups who are watching and maybe waiting for their turn. When the protocols for a 'Performance Carousel' are being followed, the groups all know that they are contributing to a whole class performance, and that everyone needs to help keep the focus on each other's performances (not just on their own). The success of a whole class performance is everyone's responsibility.

How to set it up

Groups of pupils will already have prepared their 'still images' and/or short performances (see 'still images', Section 5.12 and 'Small Group Playmaking', Section 5.15). The teacher should have informed them beforehand that they will all be performing their devised images and/or scenes afterwards as a 'Performance Carousel'.

The teacher then asks the pupils to sit on the floor 'as if' they are all on the same imaginary stage. The teacher then indicates where their imaginary audience is and then numbers the groups sequentially so that everyone knows the order in which each group will be performing. The teacher may need to remind the class that everyone is expected to keep silent and still when their group is not actually performing to ensure that the attention of the audience is always where it needs to be throughout the whole class performance. The teacher is emphasising that it is the performance that requires this, rather than the teacher.

When the imaginary stage curtain goes back (as signalled by the teacher) and the imaginary spotlight shines down on the first group, that group will start moving together in slow motion and then freeze in their starting position (a 'Freeze-frame', Section 5.11). They hold their 'Freeze-frame' still for a few seconds. If they are going to perform a short scene, then the 'Freeze-frame' will come alive and they will perform the scene. At the end of their scene, the group will freeze again together, keep the image still for a few seconds and then melt down to the floor again together, in slow motion. As Group 1 is melting slowly down to the floor, Group 2 will be slowly rising up and then freezing into their starting position (a 'Freeze-frame'). Group 2 then performs their scene, freezes its final moment (a 'Freeze-frame'), then melts back down to the floor in slow motion as Group 3 slowly rises, and so on in a process that continues until the final group has melted back down to the floor and the whole class performance is over. The teacher and class can then applaud their performance!

68 The 'Drama' strategies

Teacher tips

- Before they start devising their scenes, let the class know that their work is going to be performed immediately afterwards. Do not put the class in the position of unexpectedly having to perform.
- Use the terminology, i.e. 'Performance Carousel'. The class will soon develop an understanding of what is required of them during a 'Performance Carousel', so that you will not have to keep explaining the associated protocols each time.
- You may need to model the pace and steadiness of 'slow motion' and demonstrate the level of stillness you want to see when they are holding a 'Freeze-frame'.
- Ensure that those groups waiting to perform really do remain still and silent once the 'Performance Carousel' has started. If there are distractions such as chatter and fidgeting, then halt the performance, explain why you have done so, and then start the 'Performance Carousel' again.
- A 'Performance Carousel' can be set up without mentioning any imaginary stage or audience, but when pupils are imagining an audience, it often results in better voice projection and closer attention to the direction they are facing as they perform.
- Background music can be used to add atmosphere and help blend the scenes into one continuous performance. The volume needs to be kept at a level which ensures that any speech in the scenes is audible.

5.17 Hot-seating

What it offers

'Hot-seating' provides an opportunity for the class to question a character for a while. Gathering information directly from a character can help them to gain a deeper understanding of that character's actions, motives, feelings, opinions, and viewpoints, and help them find out what a character knows. The character is only available for questioning whilst they are on the hot-seat. Once they have left the hot-seat, what the character has said, can be noted, discussed, reflected on, and critically analysed.

'Hot-seating' gives teachers the opportunity to focus on the development of pupils' questioning skills. The character is only available to answer their questions for a short time, so the class need to make good use of that time and try to ask high-quality, well-focused questions. The teacher might give pupils time to consider their questions beforehand and perhaps work together to improve and possibly prioritise their questions before the 'hot-seating' starts.

How to set it up

The teacher can simply place a chair at the front of the room, facing the class, and inform the pupils that it is the hot-seat. When a character is sitting on that chair, they can be questioned – but once they leave the chair, they stop answering questions. The teacher might ask the pupils which character they would most like to hot-seat and ask them to explain why. The class can then hot-seat the character that most pupils want to question.

The teacher often becomes the character being hot-seated (see 'Teacher-in-Role', Section 5.2) and can knowledgably answer the pupils' questions in role, e.g. the class might hot-seat Samuel Pepys (the 'Teacher-in-Role') about his meeting with the king during the Great Fire of London, or hot-seat the 'Teacher-in-Role' as Howard Carter, just after he has seen what is in the tomb of Tutankhamun. The teacher can give historical information in role that the pupils need to know.

The teacher might sometimes invite one or more pupils to become the character who is being questioned. Each of the pupils can take a turn at sitting on the hot-seat and answering questions 'as if' they are all the one, continuous character. Alternatively, several students can be invited to stand close together 'as if' they are a single character. Any of them can answer a question that is asked, but it is advisable to have a ground rule that no-one can answer two questions in a row (see 'Collective Role', Section 5.30). This helps prevent one pupil from dominating and answering most of the questions.

The 'hot-seat' is usually an actual seat that the character comes and sits on to answer questions. However, characters can also be questioned when they are within a scene that has just been frozen (a 'Freeze-frame', Section 5.11). A character can stay in the frozen scene whilst answering questions or be invited to step out of the scene to answer questions for a while. They can then step back into the frozen scene afterwards.

In drama lessons, characters on the hot-seat answer in role. However, 'hot-seating' can be set up differently in other subject lessons, without anyone being in role. It might be that a group of pupils have researched a given topic, presented it to the class, and are then hot-seated about the topic by the rest of the class for a while. The teacher can become one of the questioners.

'Hot-seating' provides opportunities for teachers to focus on improving pupils' questioning skills. Rather than inviting a free flow of spontaneous questions to the person being hot-seated, the teacher could ask the class to work in pairs to come up with three questions that they most want to ask, and then prioritise them. The teacher might also ask the pupils to ask particular types of question, e.g. questions for clarification first and then open questions that cannot be simply answered with just a 'yes' or 'no'.

During 'hot-seating', pupils can be asked to take notes, which could be used subsequently when writing a newspaper report, diary entry, or formal recount of the interview (for example).

Teacher tips

- Do not let the 'hot-seating' go on for too long. If the quality of the questioning is declining, then bring the 'hot-seating' to a close. It is preferable to stop the 'hot-seating' when the pupils are still motivated and keen to ask more questions, rather than let them ask questions for the sake of it if they have lost interest.

Some possible 'follow-on' strategies and next steps

- Immediately after the 'hot-seating', subdivide the floor space into three stage areas, with each area representing a headed column, i.e.: 1) I know; 2) I think I know; 3) I want to know. Ask your pupils to each enter one of the three spaces in turn and voice aloud something that fits within that column.
- Following the 'hot-seating', ask your class to each jot down on individual self-adhesive labels what they know, what they think they know, and what they still want to know about the character they have just hot-seated. The jottings can then be placed in appropriately headed columns, around a 'Role on the Wall' (Section 5.29). If a character is hot-seated again at some point in the future, then the 'Role on the Wall' can be revisited and the content reconsidered.
- After they have been hot-seated, maybe ask the character to stand in the centre of a class circle. In turn, invite pupils to cross the circle and say something about (or to) the character as they pass by them (see 'Passing Thoughts', Section 5.24).
- After a character has been hot-seated, get the character to stand in the centre of a class circle and ask the pupils to physically position themselves in relation to the character in a meaningful way. As each pupil gets into position, they can say what they are thinking and/or feeling about the character (see 'Proxemics', Section 5.25).

5.18 Thought-tracking

What it offers

'Thought-tracking' enables what a character is silently thinking to be voiced and shared publicly. What a fictional character is thinking may not always be congruent with what a character is saying and doing (for various reasons). Once this disparity has been revealed through 'thought-tracking', the reasons for it can be considered.

'Thought-tracking' can help pupils to gain a deeper knowledge and understanding of a character's feelings, actions, motives, and intentions, e.g. a soldier might appear very brave but if we can listen to his inner thoughts, we might discover that the soldier is terrified and struggling to appear brave. In a scene involving bullying, the gang members may appear to be unified in their support of a ring-leader, but if we 'thought-track' those present in the scene and listen to their inner thoughts, we might find that some of the gang are empathising with the victim but are too frightened of the bully to reveal this.

Teachers can use 'thought-tracking' as a strategy in any subject lesson. A class discussion can be halted for a while to give individual pupils the opportunity to voice and share their personal thoughts and opinions about any issue or subject matter at that particular moment, e.g. during a class discussion about whether mobile phones should be allowed in classrooms or not.

How to set it up

In a drama lesson, the teacher might freeze a scene that is underway and say that they will now 'thought-track' the fictional (or historical) characters within the scene, thus enabling everyone to hear what the various characters in the scene are thinking. If it is a class discussion that is underway, then the teacher will halt the discussion to thought-track what some (or all) of the pupils in turn are thinking at that moment about the subject under discussion.

When 'thought-tracking', the teacher can touch the shoulders of pupils, to signal that it is their turn to speak. However, rather than touching pupils' shoulders, some teachers may prefer to just stand beside pupils in turn or use some other signal. For example, some teachers have made giant, empty thought bubbles out of large bits of card and they hold them close to the pupil when it is their turn to speak their thoughts. This is like the way thought bubbles are used in comics and graphic novels.

Some possible 'follow-on' strategies and next steps

- To compare what a fictional character is saying publicly, with what that character is thinking privately, you can make and use both large speech bubbles and large thought bubbles. Hold up the speech bubble and then the thought bubble by the character's head (or vice versa), so that the class can hear what the character is both saying and thinking at a particular moment.

- A character's thoughts can be jotted down on individual self-adhesive labels and placed inside a giant thought bubble. This can then become a resource for pupils if they are subsequently asked to write a soliloquy or monologue for that character. Alternatively, the thoughts can be stuck around a 'Role on the Wall' (Section 5.29).
- If there is a difference between what a character is thinking inwardly and publicly saying, then the class can be invited to question the character (see 'Hot-seating', Section 5.17).
- The thoughts that are vocally gathered through 'thought-tracking' can subsequently be presented as a 'Thought Collage' (Section 5.33).

5.19 Conscience Alley

What it offers

A 'Conscience Alley' helps the class to think about, speak, and hear some of the conflicting thoughts that might be going on within a character's conscience at a particular moment. This strategy is often used when there are characters in fiction (or historical characters) who are struggling with a moral dilemma and having a crisis of conscience.

How to set it up

The pupils stand in two straight lines facing each other, a metre or two apart. The opposite lines represent the opposing thoughts battling within the character's conscience at a moment in time. The character (who is often represented by the 'Teacher-in-Role') walks slowly between the lines and will linger long enough by each pupil to ensure they have enough time to voice and share an inner thought 'as if' they are one of the voices of the character's conscience.

Teacher tips

- Remind the class that it is not just the character that needs to hear whatever is being said during a 'Conscience Alley'. Whatever is being said by anyone needs to be loud enough to be heard by the whole class.
- Remember that the distance between the lines and the character might have an impact on how connected the pupils feel to the character who is passing by (and vice versa).

Linked activities and variations

- The character can pass between the lines more than once, thereby giving each pupil more than one opportunity to speak as a voice from the character's conscience.
- The character can pass between the lines more than once, but the first time, the character just listens to each voice in turn. The second time, the character verbally responds.
- The character can pass between the lines more than once but the first time slowly, so that each voice is clearly heard in turn, and the second time hurriedly, so that the voices overlap. This can suggest that the character is getting increasingly stressed by the overlapping, conflicting thoughts.
- The two lines can become continuous lines, thereby giving the pupils several turns, speaking as the character's conscience. Once pupils have spoken to the character, they immediately break away from the front of their line and rejoin it at the other end (as happens in country dancing). The character keeps on walking between the lines which are ongoing, as they are reforming continuously. The continuity of voices might suggest that the character's conflicting thoughts are relentless.

5.20 Decision Alley

What it offers

As the name suggests, a character going through a 'Decision Alley' has a decision to make. The pupils in the two different lines represent the voices within a decision-maker's mind. This can also be the case in a 'Conscience Alley' (Section 5.19), but not all decisions are a matter of conscience, as some decisions are more operational than personal. During a 'Decision Alley', the voices in one line try to move the decision-maker towards or away from making a particular decision. The pupils in both lines all get an opportunity to advise the character one way or the other. The voices in the opposing lines can state either the pros or cons of making a particular decision. Regardless of which line pupils are standing in, they will all hear what is being said by everyone, and every pupil will have had the chance to speak and be listened to.

How to set it up

The class is split in half, with the pupils facing each other in two straight lines that are about 1–2 metres apart. The teacher tells the pupils whether the line they are standing in will be persuading or dissuading the character from imminently making a particular decision.

The character (often the 'Teacher-in-Role') then walks between the lines and listens to each pupil in turn. The character will listen to the conflicting voices and then usually make their decision once they reach the end of the 'Decision Alley'. They might also tell the pupils what they heard that particularly influenced their decision.

Some possible 'follow-on' strategies and next steps

- The two lines can be considered as two columns. What the voices in each line said can afterwards be written onto self-adhesive labels and placed under two headed columns on a large sheet of paper (or recorded in columns on a class whiteboard). This can then become a central resource, if the pupils are subsequently asked to write a balanced argument or write persuasively for or against the decision.
- The pupils in each line can gather afterwards, in two separate groups. Each group in turn can then improvise a 'Voice Collage' (Section 5.32) together, with the pupils drawing on what they each of them said to the character in the 'Decision Alley'.

5.21 Thought Tunnel

What it offers

The types of thinking used and voiced within a 'Thought Tunnel' need not necessarily be confined to the types of thinking that are associated with matters of conscience and/or decision-making (as in a 'Conscience Alley', Section 5.19 or 'Decision Alley', Section 5.20). A 'Thought Tunnel' offers the opportunity for each pupil in turn to use and voice any type of thinking (in role or personal). The teacher can focus the pupils on the type of thinking they want to hear voiced in a 'Thought Tunnel'. The pupils' thinking can be focused on something real or fictitious, e.g. a real or fictional character, situation, setting, event, incident, or issue, and the class need not necessarily be tasked with trying to influence the thinking of others. The person walking through the 'Thought Tunnel' is usually the teacher and need not be in role. They still can be the trigger for each of the pupils' voiced thoughts as they pass by.

How to set it up

A 'Thought Tunnel' uses the same configuration as a 'Conscience Alley' and a 'Decision Alley', i.e. two straight lines of pupils facing each other. It also invites pupils in turn to speak their thoughts (in role or personal) as someone (usually the teacher) walks between the lines.

The teacher can invite a free flow of pupils' thoughts on a given topic or might choose to frame the activity in a way that requires the class to use a particular type of thinking. For example, the pupils could be asked to voice a happy personal memory in turn or share something that they are wondering about. The thoughts spoken in the 'Thought Tunnel' could be focused by the teacher on something that the pupils have just been learning about or have recently seen or read.

5.22 Corridor of Voices

What it offers

A 'Corridor of Voices' uses the same configuration as a 'Conscience Alley', 'Decision Alley', or 'Thought Tunnel', but as its name suggests, it offers great flexibility in relation to what the voices might be talking about. For example, the pupils might be asked to voice in turn their suggestions about how to solve a problem, or might each be recalling a fact about a given subject, or adding the next sentence to whatever the previous person has just said, or each asking a question to the passer-by, etc. Every pupil gets an opportunity to speak. If the teacher is the passer-by, they might choose to linger longer by certain pupils, thus giving them a little longer to be listened to by the class. The pupils' voices might be saying something in turn about a fictional or real issue, situation, event, person, or incident, for example.

Some possible curriculum links

- In a drama or English lesson, it might be a fictional character walking through the corridor, with the voices (in or out of role) talking to or about the character as they pass by. In a History lesson, the character passing by might be historical and the voices might each be giving a fact or personal opinion about the character. In a Geography lesson, the voices might all state one fact about a country that the pupil discovered by searching online during enquiry-based homework. In a mathematics lesson, the voices in the corridor might all be saying the next number in a numerical sequence, e.g. each pupil might be adding three when it is their turn. In a PSHE and relationships lesson, the voices might be intentionally reassuring or restorative towards the passer-by (possibly the 'Teacher-in-Role' (Section 5.2) as a distressed fictional character).

How to set it up

The pupils need to stand in two lines and face each other, with space enough between the lines for someone (usually the teacher) to walk between the lines. The lines represent a corridor and the voices heard will be those of each pupil speaking in turn as the passer-by is nearest to them. The teacher tells the pupils what their verbal task is going to be, and whether or not they will be speaking to the passer-by directly. The class may need to be reminded that their voices need to be heard by everyone and not just by the passer-by.

5.23 'Thought-walk'

What it offers

'Thought-walking' gives pupils an opportunity to speak an unrehearsed, internal monologue aloud, to themselves, without the pressure of being listened to by their teacher or peers. The pupils walk around the room, talking to themselves about a given subject, with nobody listening. 'Thought-walking' can help pupils to recall information and clarify their thinking. This is helpful in itself, but 'thought-walking' can also be used as a form of preparation or rehearsal. Having talked to themselves about a subject first, pupils are usually more confident when talking to (or with) others about the subject afterwards. 'Thought-walking' can also be helpful if they are going to write about a subject afterwards.

How to set it up

The pupils all stand in a space. At a given signal from the teacher, they all start walking around the room in various directions and keeping their distance from each other. As they walk around, they speak their inner thoughts aloud, to themselves, about whatever the given subject is.

Variation

- It may be helpful sometimes to say that they can stand still and think from time to time, and then resume their walking and talking. You will need to judge whether standing still sometimes is helpful or not, as pupils should not stop and then start listening to others who are 'thought-walking'.

Some possible 'follow-on' strategies and next steps

- Having spoken to themselves during a 'thought-walk', they can then be asked to recount what they have been saying, to an imaginary partner. This is a possible 'next step' before talking to (and with) a real partner.

5.24 Passing Thoughts

What it offers

'Passing Thoughts' is a strategy that gives pupils the opportunity to share aloud, in turn, what they are each thinking about a centrally placed character (or they might be asked to say what the character could be thinking). The character is usually in the centre, with the class standing in a circle around the character.

This strategy can be used in any subject lesson, as the focus need not always be a character. Instead, an issue, statement, or idea can be written onto a centrally placed piece of paper and become the focus of the pupil's thoughts and comments. For example, a provocative statement such as, 'The voting age should be lowered to 16' can be placed centrally and the pupils can cross the circle in random order, saying what they each think about the statement as they pass by it.

How to set it up

The class stands in a circle with the character, issue, statement, or idea, positioned/placed in the centre. In random order, the pupils cross the circle in turn and say what they personally think about it. Not every pupil has to take a turn, and some pupils may decide to have more than one turn (but no pupil should take two turns in a row).

When 'Passing Thoughts' are used in drama lessons, the teacher might ask the pupils to speak their thoughts directly to the character as they pass by him/her or maybe to speak the thoughts of the character. Instead of the character standing in the centre, an object that represents the character can be placed there, e.g. a piece of their clothing or an empty chair. Symbolic objects and written statements can also be placed centrally in other subject lessons, e.g. a globe, when sharing thoughts about a global issue.

Some possible 'follow-on' strategies and next steps

- 'Passing Thoughts' can be used just prior to a class discussion on the character, issue, idea, or statement.
- The thoughts that were shared during the activity can be jotted down and displayed afterwards. If the pupils' thoughts and comments were about a character, then they can be written on self-adhesive labels and stuck around a 'Role on the Wall' (Section 5.29). If the thoughts were about a statement, issue, or idea, then they could be written inside a class thought bubble or speech bubble.

5.25 Proxemics

What it offers

The physical space between people carries meaning, both in everyday life and on stage. Pupils are taught in drama that the space between characters has meaning and can be an indicator of the characters' relationships and their feelings towards each other.

The class can be asked to consider what they think and feel about a character and then communicate this intentionally, through their intentional spatial positioning, in relation to the character. In other curriculum subjects, pupils can be asked to position themselves in turn, in relation to a centrally placed idea, statement, or issue which may be represented in some concrete way, e.g. by placing a symbolic object, image, or written statement centrally.

How to set it up

The class stands in a circle, with the character in the centre. Having considered what they think and feel about the character, each pupil in turn positions themselves - spatially and meaningfully - in relation to the character. They can be asked to justify and explain their relative positioning, using a sentence stem such as, 'I am standing here because . . .'.

Some possible 'follow-on' strategies and next steps

- 'Proxemics' can precede a class discussion and/or debate about the centrally placed character, idea, statement, or issue. Afterwards, the pupils can be asked to position themselves again, and some may have shifted their positions because of the discussion.
- The pupils' spatial positioning in relation to a character can subsequently be recorded using a 'Role on the Wall' (Section 5.29). Whatever each pupil said can be written afterwards on individual self-adhesive labels and then positioned similarly, in relation to an outline of the character, that has been drawn on a large sheet of paper.
- If the pupils have already positioned themselves spatially in relation to a central statement, issue, idea, or image, they can then each write what they said on self-adhesive labels and then position them similarly, on a large sheet of paper, that has the written statement, idea, issue, or image centrally positioned.

5.26 Spectrum of Difference/Spectrogram

What it offers

A 'Spectrum of Difference' can be used to show where all the pupils stand on a particular issue, both literally and metaphorically. Each pupil decides where to position themselves on an imaginary line. The opposite ends of the line represent the opposite ends of the spectrum on a given issue. Not only does each pupil have to consider where they personally stand on the given issue, they also have to justify and explain their positioning to each other and the class. They also get to see where others stand on the same issue and hear their explanations and justifications, too.

How to set it up

The teacher indicates where an imaginary line starts and finishes, and explains that the opposite ends of the line represent different ends of the same spectrum in relation to a given issue, e.g. one end of the line could represent 'Workers in emergency services should definitely be allowed to strike' and the other end of the line could represent 'Workers in emergency services should never be allowed to strike'. This is a 'Spectrum of Difference'. Each pupil then places themselves on the spectrum, showing where they personally stand in relation to the issue statements at either end. They can be asked to all place themselves silently on the spectrum at the same time. Alternatively, they might be asked to enter in turn, position themselves on the line, then justify and explain their positioning to everyone, possibly using the sentence stem 'I am standing here because . . .'

If the pupils have together silently positioned themselves on the spectrum, they will then need to talk with each other to check whether or not they are in the right position. Each pupil can talk with the pupils who are standing either side of them, then decide whether they need to change places on the spectrum or not. Once everyone thinks they are in their correct position, this can be checked if each pupil briefly explains to the class where they stand on the issue.

Linked activities and variations

- In drama lessons, pupils are sometimes asked to imagine that the line that they are all standing on is a tightrope high up in the air. Whenever pupils change places along the tightrope (the 'Spectrum of Difference'), they need to physically help each other to move along the tightrope so that nobody falls off!

5.27 Move if . . .

What it offers

This strategy is sometimes used at the start of lessons to get pupils connecting personally with some of the themes in the forthcoming lesson. It gets them remembering and briefly re-engaging with real-life past experiences that may resonate during the lesson. The strategy also enables pupils to see that some of their peers may have had some similar life experiences to their own. The teacher can join in, too, if they wish.

How to set it up

The class stand in a circle. The teacher calls out a sentence that starts with the sentence stem, 'Move if . . .'. Whenever the sentence that is spoken, is true for any pupil, they respond by silently walking across to the other side of the circle. The number of pupils crossing the circle in response to each sentence can vary significantly, and sometimes the sentence is not true for any of the class, so nobody moves.

Before a lesson about human migration, for example, the teacher might say the following, for example.

> 'Move if you have ever moved house'.
> 'Move if you have ever lived in another country'.
> 'Move if you speak more than one language'.

Before a lesson about climate change, the teacher might say the following, for example.

> 'Move if you have ever flown in an aeroplane'.
> 'Move if you have a wood burner at home'.
> 'Move if you have thrown something into a recycling bin today'.

Before a lesson about Shakespeare's *Macbeth*, the teacher could say the following, for example.

> 'Move if you have ever been on a sleepover'.
> 'Move if you have ever been to Scotland'.
> 'Move if you have ever been inside a castle'.

5.28 Freeze if . . .

What it offers

The purposes of 'Freeze if . . .' are like those of 'Move if . . .', but the pupils are all moving around the room rather than standing in a circle. If the teacher calls out a sentence that applies to any pupil personally, then they freeze. They stay frozen until some other sentence is called out by the teacher that does not apply to them. All the sentences that the teacher calls will have some relevance to the forthcoming lesson.

How to set it up

The teacher needs to have a few sentences ready that are linked to the themes of the forthcoming lesson. The teacher then asks the pupils to walk around the room and to keep their distance from each other. They will need to change directions at times to avoid all just walking around in a class circle. From time to time, the teacher will call out one of the sentences. If the sentence holds true for any of the pupils, then they need to immediately freeze and remain still until they hear a different sentence spoken by the teacher that does not apply to them personally.

Before a lesson about the Great Fire of London, the teacher might say the following, for example.

> 'Freeze if you have ever been to London'.
> 'Freeze if you have ever walked along a cobbled street'.
> 'Freeze if you own a diary'.

Before a lesson about *Theseus and the Minotaur*, the teacher might say the following, for example.

> 'Freeze if you have ever been to Greece'.
> 'Freeze if you have ever been on a ship'.
> 'Freeze if you have ever walked through a maze'.

Before a lesson about theatre, the teacher could say the following, for example.

> 'Freeze if you have ever read a playscript'.
> 'Freeze if you have ever been to a theatre'.
> 'Freeze if you have ever acted in a play'.

Variation

Having carried out 'Freeze if . . .', the teacher can make it more challenging by replaying it differently, i.e. 'This time, if the sentence is true for you, keep walking. If the sentence is not true for you, then freeze'. The pupils need to really concentrate once this opposite rule is applied.

5.29 Role on the Wall

What it offers

'Role on the Wall' is a strategy for visually organising and mapping information about a character. If the teacher adds headed columns, then this will help focus the pupils' inter-thinking around certain aspects of the character, e.g. the character's thoughts, words, and actions. When pupils all add information to a 'Role on the Wall', they each need to be able to justify and explain what each of them has added (if asked to do so). This often stimulates class discussions about the character. The 'Role on the Wall' is a visual resource that belongs to the class. It can be reviewed from time to time, as more becomes known about a character. The advantage of writing information and thoughts about a character on self-adhesive labels (rather than directly onto the 'Role on the Wall') is that whatever has been written on each label can be reviewed from time to time and may then be repositioned or even removed once more becomes known about the character. If a chronological series of 'roles on the wall' are completed for the same character, then it can highlight a character's development.

How to set it up

An outline of the character's body is drawn on a big sheet of paper. The pupils are then asked to individually write different bits of information about the character on separate self-adhesive labels. The teacher may have drawn some headed columns around the 'Role on the Wall' (Table 5.2) to focus the pupils' attention specifically on which column certain pieces of information belong in.

Table 5.2 'Role on the Wall' (optional columns)

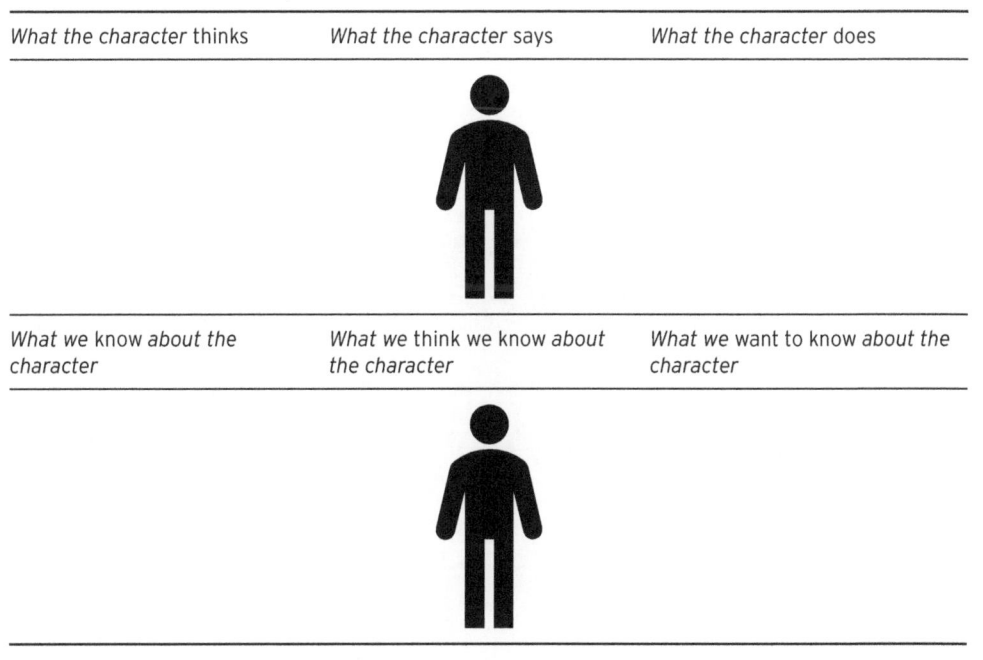

What the character thinks	*What the character* says	*What the character* does
What we know *about the character*	*What we think we know about the character*	*What we* want to know *about the character*

In turn, each pupil then reads aloud what they have written on one of their labels, then sticks it in an appropriate position on the 'Role on the Wall'. As the labels are being added in turn, discussion might be stimulated but it might be that the teacher holds back any challenge or discussion until all pupils have placed their labels.

Linked activities and variations

- The pupils can be asked to write straight onto the 'Role on the Wall' rather than onto self-adhesive labels. They can be invited to write on the 'Role on the Wall' in turn or simultaneously.
- All the self-adhesive labels with information on them can be initially stuck in random order, all around the 'Role on the Wall'. The pupils can then be asked to sort the labels and reposition them meaningfully and appropriately, e.g. 'He is very clever' could be moved and stuck onto the character's forehead. If the teacher has added columns, then the pupils might all be moving each other's labels into the correct column(s).
- A row of paper dolls can be cut from a sheet of folded paper to produce a series of small empty 'roles on the wall'. Information can be recorded about the character at different points in time. When considered chronologically, this can help pupils if they are tracking a character's development.

5.30 Collective Role

What it offers

The 'Collective Role' strategy enables several pupils to improvise in turn, 'as if' they are a single character. This gives them the opportunity to all input equally into the spontaneous portrayal of a real or fictional character. To do this effectively, they have to listen carefully to each other so that what they character says is consistent. If it is an historical character they are collaboratively improvising, they must have some prior knowledge of the character and maintain a respect for evidence during the improvisation. Also, if the character they are improvising in turn is fictional but comes from an existing novel or story, then they can still be expected to take into account whatever they already know about the fictional character during their 'Collective Role'.

How to set it up

Instruct a group of 4-6 pupils to position themselves together, 'as if' they are one character. Each of them may only speak one sentence at a time, in role as the character. No-one may speak two sentences in a row as the character. The order in which they all speak their sentences can be random, but the content of must be consistent. Each pupil in the group can take several turns at adding a sentence. This shares the responsibility for what the character says overall and helps prevent one pupil from dominating.

5.31 Choral Speaking

What it offers

'Choral Speaking' is a collaborative and performative experience with groups of pupils (or the whole class), exploring and devising various ways of performing pieces of verse and prose together. To do this meaningfully and well, the pupils need to get to know and understand the text. They can interact with each other and use accompanying movements, expressions, gestures, and even sound effects.

'Choral Speaking' can be in unison, with everyone speaking together throughout, or the text can be divided up so that at various times, there are different groups or individuals speaking. Some pupils might be just repeatedly joining in with a chorus. The class could simply be asked to sit in a circle, with each pupil in turn reading the next part of a text and then passing it on.

'Choral Speaking' performances are usually rehearsed and refined to communicate mood, atmosphere, and meaning effectively. The pupils know that they have a collective responsibility for the success of the choral performance, and this can lead to pupils feeling a sense of personal responsibility and belonging.

How to set it up

There are many ways in which Choral Speaking can be set up. It helps if all pupils can see a copy of the text and be given sufficient time to read it through to themselves first and then read it aloud to themselves, too, with nobody listening. They might then be asked to highlight, underline, and/or annotate parts of the text to help guide them vocally. For example, they might have a paper copy of the text and highlight the parts that they will be joining in with, underline the key words, and clearly mark where the pauses need to be. The teacher usually models reading the text aloud first, so that everyone hears the whole text and the correct pronunciation of any unfamiliar words. The teacher and class might then read the whole text in unison before subdividing it and maybe experimenting with it vocally in various ways, then rehearsing and performing it for an imaginary audience – and maybe for a real audience too.

Linked activities and variations

- The pupils are seated in a circle. Each in turn speaks only the next line of the text, until the reading is complete. This might just be the initial reading by the class, before the teacher allocates different parts of the text to different pupils or groups of pupils.
- One person reads the text aloud and everyone else just joins in the chorus, or only joins in with certain words or phrases.
- Characters that speak within the text can be spoken by individual pupils during the reading, with the rest of the text being spoken in unison.
- Pace, pitch, volume, and silence can be varied and experimented with for meaning and effect.

- Solo voices can speak particularly significant lines and then multiple voices can echo them. Alternatively, everyone voices in unison the particularly significant lines (which may have already been underlined).
- Vocal sound effects and/or bodily percussion sounds can be added as an accompaniment at various points.
- Meaningful gestures, movements, and interactions can be added for emphasis.

5.32 Voice Collage

What it offers

A 'Voice Collage' is a one-off improvised performance, consisting of words, lines, and/or phrases that are spoken aloud and which have usually been selected by the pupils themselves, maybe from some type of text they are studying, e.g. a playscript, historic speech, or poem. Alternatively, they could be words, phrases, or lines of their own creation, or ones that they have just spoken during a drama 'Improvisation' or devised scene. A 'Voice Collage' gives pupils the opportunity to select what they consider significant enough to include and then experiment with it vocally, repeatedly and collaboratively, 'in the moment' and for effect.

How to set it up

Each pupil decides on the word, phrase, or sentence that they will be contributing to the 'Voice Collage'. They usually close their eyes during a 'Voice Collage', as this helps them focus on what is being said (and how it is being said), without any visual distractions. Once the teacher signals the start of the 'Voice Collage' (maybe by being the first voice), then any pupil may speak their word, sentence, or phrase, whenever and as often as they wish. Pupils may also choose to remain silent at times, judging when, how, and how often to contribute, for overall effect. The pupils need to remain aware of each other's voices throughout.

A 'Voice Collage' usually starts quietly (with maybe just one or two voices), then more voices gradually are heard. The volume and pace rises slowly to a crescendo, then the voices fall away gradually, becoming fewer and quieter until eventually there is silence. The pupils keep their eyes closed until the teacher signals that everyone can open their eyes again.

A 'Voice Collage' is usually just a one-off improvised performance with no rehearsal and no real audience. However, a 'Voice Collage' could be improvised first then refined, rehearsed, and performed for an imaginary or real audience.

5.33 Thought Collage

What it offers

A 'Thought Collage' is like a 'Voice Collage' (Section 5.32) except that it is thoughts that are being spoken within an improvised, one-off performance, rather than utterances. The thoughts that pupils select and use to create a 'Thought Collage' might have been revealed by using other strategies, such as 'Thought-tracking' (Section 5.18) or during a 'Conscience Alley' (Section 5.19). The thoughts voiced in the collage need not necessarily be those of a fictional character they are learning about in English or drama. The pupils' personal thoughts about a given subject, theme, situation, issue, or idea can be brought together in a 'Thought Collage'.

How to set it up

The pupils each decide on a thought that they will contribute verbally from time to time during the 'Thought Collage'. The teacher then explains that when the 'Thought Collage' starts, anyone may speak their thought aloud (or part of it), whenever and as often as they wish, and in any way that they consider to be effective and fitting. Their thoughts, however, need to come in one or two at a time initially (rather than starting simultaneously). They will be gradually building up to a crescendo of voiced thoughts, then their thoughts need to gradually fall away and become quieter, so that the volume of the improvised performance slowly decreases and ends in silence. The pupils need to keep their eyes closed throughout and not open them again until instructed to do so by the teacher.

The directions the teacher gives can be adjusted according to the subject matter. For example, if the 'Thought Collage' is about something that is cyclical, then it could start all over again, whereas if the 'Thought Collage' is based on something dangerous and/or terminal, then it might end gradually or suddenly to reflect this.

5.34 Sound Collage

What it offers

A 'Sound Collage' is an improvised or devised short performance of sounds. The sounds may be connected to a text or image, a theme, issue, situation, character, or historical event, for example. Whatever the stimulus, the pupils will be focusing on sounds that are evident or suggested by the stimulus. They then set about finding ways of producing some of these sounds together. The pupils might just use their voices and bodies to make sounds but might be invited by the teacher to use available objects and/or instruments, too.

The teacher offers a stimulus (such as a text or image) and asks the pupils to focus on the sounds that are evident within it and/or implied. The teacher might also invite pupils to suggest some other appropriate sounds that could be added. Focusing on sounds, linked with something that the pupils are studying, can help make it more memorable.

How to set it up

The teacher provides a stimulus, e.g. a narrative poem or an image. If the stimulus is a text, the pupils can be asked to underline anything within the text that specifically refers to or suggests sound. If the stimulus is an image, then they will be looking for anything that is associated with sound and maybe listing it.

The pupils can then be asked to get into small groups to gather and agree the sounds they have noted, i.e. which words and phrases they have underlined in a text or listed in relation to the image. For example, If the class were studying the opening of *The Highwayman* by Alfred Noyes (1906), for example, then they might underline such words and phrases as gusty wind, hooves clattering and crashing, the tap of a whip on shutters, a tune being whistled, creaking, galloping, etc.

Once the group has gathered the sounds, they can each take one or more of them and start finding ways of making them, using their bodies and voices and maybe using objects from around the room, too. Instruments might sometimes also be available to them. The teacher needs to make it clear that the groups are not being asked to sequence the sounds narratively, as they appear in the poem. They are expected to play with the sounds in an exploratory way together and devise an interesting collage with the sounds that the groups will subsequently perform for each other as a 'Sound Collage'.

As a 'Sound Collage' performance consists only of sounds, the audience may be asked to close their eyes whilst they listen, as this avoids visual distractions. The teacher might decide to let the performing groups decide where they want their audience to be and whether they want the audience to close their eyes. For example, the performers might choose to position themselves around their audience, thus surrounding their listeners with sounds. The groups will each have devised different 'sound collages' from the same stimulus.

Linked activities and variations

- After groups have performed their 'Sound Collages' for each other, they might sometimes be asked to improvise a whole class 'Sound Collage', again using the sounds they made.
- The 'Sound Collage' can be performed seamlessly by groups in turn, using a 'Performance Carousel' (Section 5.16).
- Thought, sound, and voice collages can be combined to produce a collage of words and sounds.

5.35 Soundscape

What it offers

A 'Soundscape' is made up of a combination of sounds that are put together with intent to suggest a particular location, mood, or atmosphere. A 'Soundscape' (like a film soundtrack) can often evoke an emotional response when heard. Creating an appropriate and effective soundscape requires pupils to consider a range of possible auditory content then work critically and creatively together as a team to select and make sounds collaboratively that achieve their intended outcome.

How to set it up

Soundscapes are usually generated by groups of pupils. The class may be asked to focus on the natural and/or human-made sounds within a given text, image, setting, or scene (for example). They will first need to consider some appropriate sounds and agree which to include. They then need to find ways of making these sounds, maybe just using their voices and bodies, although the teacher might choose to also give them access to objects and/or instruments. The class might also be given some opportunities to include sounds and sound effects that they have found online.

Groups usually perform their soundscapes for each other. One way of performing a soundscape is for the listening audience to be seated together on the floor (with their eyes closed) and with the performers surrounding them. This provides a more immersive listening experience.

5.36 Sound Story

What it offers

A sequence of sounds can be made by groups of pupils (or by the teacher), that suggest a scene or story to those who are listening. The sounds might be intentionally sequenced to suggest a known story, or a 'Sound Story' that the pupils who are making the sounds have created. Even random sounds can start to suggest scenes and stories in the minds of listeners. A 'Sound Story' can be performed by just using voices and bodies, or the pupils can also be invited to use objects and instruments to make sounds, too.

How to set it up

Groups of pupils can be asked to make and perform a series of sounds together that tell a story. Alternatively, the groups can each be allocated a different episode from a story that they all know. When performed chronologically, they will end up telling the whole story through sound. The groups might be asked to use their voices and/or bodies to make all the sounds, or they could be invited to use objects and/or instruments. They might sometimes be invited to search for sound effects online, then sequence and record them to tell a story.

The listening 'blind' classmates will need to use their imaginations to come up with some possible stories, suggested by the sequence of sounds to which they have just listened.

Teacher tip

- Make sure the listeners know that the sounds are telling a story, as they will then be ready to look for narrative connections.

Linked activities and variations

- The teacher can produce a sound sequence for their class that individual pupils can then create their own stories with. The class can then get into pairs of small groups to recount their various stories to each other before going on to write their stories.

5.37 Sensory Journey

What it offers

This is an opportunity for pupils to lead a 'blind' partner on a journey through an imaginary setting. A 'Sensory Journey' requires the blind partner to trust their lead partner safety-wise as they guide them around, verbally and/or physically by the arm. The lead partner describes the imaginary setting vividly to their blind partner as they move around, and looks out for objects and materials that they can get their 'blind' partner to touch, 'as if' they are something else, e.g. the 'blind' partner might be guided to touch a window pane and the lead partner might say, 'Behind this glass is a painting of the king. He looks very powerful'.

How to set it up

The pupils are divided into pairs. One pupil will close their eyes and their partner will take them by the arm and guide them (verbally and/or physically) through an imaginary setting. The setting could be original, or could be one based on a relevant text or image. The lead partner needs to describe the setting vividly and might also mention characters and incidents in connection with it. On the journey through the setting, they will get their 'blind' partner to touch objects and tell them that they are something else, e.g. the blind partner could be led to touch a wooden table and their partner might say, 'This is the table that Beowulf feasted at. The strong hands that ripped off Grendel's arm have touched this wood'. The partners should then swap so that they both get a turn at leading and being led blind.

Teacher tip

- This activity is improvised, so no preparation or rehearsal is required. However, teachers may wish to give the class a few moments to glance around the room first and notice some objects or materials that they might use when leading.

Linked activities and variations

- Talking descriptively about an imaginary setting first can be a helpful step towards writing about it afterwards.
- The blind partner usually just follows their partner silently and listens, but might sometimes be allowed to talk with their guide during the journey.

5.38 Telephone Conversations

What it offers

This is a strategy that enables two people to have an improvised dialogue without looking at each other. In drama lessons, the dialogue usually happens 'in role', but this strategy could be used out of role, too, in any subject lesson. A range of purposeful conversations can be improvised between people that each require different types of speech, e.g. an improvised phone call to the emergency services or two best friends confiding in each other by phone. Not looking at people when talking with them removes the possibility of each reading the other's facial expressions and seeing their gestures. This keeps the pairs' attention only on what is being spoken and heard.

How to set it up

The pupils get into pairs, space out in the room and sit back to back. One pupil supposedly rings the other, usually by imitating the sound of a telephone ringing. Their partner answers the imaginary phone and their improvised conversation begins. It continues until one of them hangs up or the teacher halts the activity. As the pairs will naturally finish their phone conversations at different times, those pairs who have completed their calls need to sit still and be silent until everyone has finished talking or has been 'cut off' by the teacher.

The pupils need to know whether they will be talking in role or as themselves. They also need to be clear about the purpose of their phone call, e.g. 'You are phoning your best friend to talk about some bullying you have just seen', or 'You are a newspaper reporter interviewing someone whose home will soon be lost to coastal erosion'.

Some possible 'follow-on' strategies and next steps

- If the teacher wants the class to listen in afterwards to parts of each other's phone calls, then they could use the 'Eavesdropping' (Section 5.5) strategy next.

5.39 Drama Maps

What it offers

'Drama Maps' can be made of real or fictional places, and they can be created individually or collaboratively. In drama, maps may be drawn either in or out of role, and they often pictorially represent the place where the drama will be (or is) happening. If the map is one that is created by the pupils collaboratively, then they acquire a sense of shared ownership and gain communal knowledge and understanding of the place they have depicted on the map.

There are different types of maps. Some depict natural landscape features such as rivers and mountains, and others include human-made features which may be of cultural, communal, and/or personal significance, e.g. churches, homes, schools, parks, etc. Even a few details on a map can stimulate pupils' imaginations and lead to them adding further details to their collectively created map.

Maps can also be drawn of fictional places that the pupils are reading about in stories and novels. As the pupils get to know more about the place and the people during their reading, they can add further details to the map.

How to set it up

The pupils are sitting or standing in a circle. A large sheet of paper (or long roll of paper) is placed centrally, with plenty of coloured felt tip pens available. The teacher explains that together the pupils are going to draw a map of a fictional place within which the drama will take place. The teacher might ask them to draw and label features of the natural landscape first, then ask them to add public buildings, their homes, and finally, a place that is of particular significance to them personally (in role). They might just label what they each put on the map but could be asked to also write a relevant sentence by it. If the map they are drawing together is based on a story they are reading, then whatever they put on the map needs to be evident in the story and the relevant sentences they add might come from the text.

Some possible 'follow-on' strategies and next steps

- Ask the pupils to stand either side of the map on the floor. Explain that you will walk on and around the map. Whenever you are standing close to something on the map, the person who drew it will give you some information about it.
- Alternatively, you can ask the class to make sound effects that fit with whatever you are closest to as you move around the map, e.g. if you are standing close to a forest on the map, then there may be sounds of a wolf howling, wind rustling the leaves, birds, etc. (see Soundscape, Section 5.35).

Further suggestions

- Instead of drawing maps together on paper, the pupils can construct a 3D map collaboratively, using sheets of material, boxes, books, and any other available objects, e.g. a blue sheet might be positioned to represent the sea, a green sheet of material placed

over books might represent an island in the sea, small boxes can be added as buildings, etc. Features can then be labelled on the 3D map. This way of creating a fictional setting together at the start of a whole class drama, was sometimes used by Dorothy Heathcote, a renowned educator and a pioneer of drama as a learning medium.
- Some children's picture books contain a pictorial map of the story setting, e.g. the Katie Morag books by Mairi Hedderwick (1985), include a map of the fictional Isle of Struay. If stories that the pupils are reading do not have an accompanying map, then the class can be invited to draw one together that fits the story.
- In various stories and picture books for children, characters have an aerial view of the land at some point. A character might climb high, (*Jack and the Beanstalk'*), or can magically fly (*Peter Pan*, 2021), or travels in a space rocket (*Noah and the Space Ark*, 1997), or goes up in a hot-air balloon (*Tom and the Island of Dinosaurs*, 1995). If the pupils close their eyes and imagine that they are the character looking down, they can be invited to imagine and say aloud what they can see, each using the sentence stem, 'I can see . . .'. They then open their eyes together and start mapping together the aerial view they have collectively described.
- Some stories and narrative poems describe journeys that the class can simultaneously re-enact using 'follow my leader' or 'Active Storytelling' (Section 5.9). The journey can then be pictorially mapped. For example, if the class is reading Tennyson's *Lady of Shalott*, her final journey from the tower, down the river to the quay at Camelot can be mimed and then mapped, with lines from the poem then placed at appropriate points on the map.

98 *The 'Drama' strategies*

5.40 Story Maps

What it offers

'Story Maps' can be drawn and used to sequentially map existing stories or as a way of planning new stories. A 'Story Map' is mainly pictorial and usually linear in form. It makes visible the bare bones of a narrative in an organised, sequential way. It usually consists of a series of simply drawn pictures, with just a few words or phrases jotted next to and/or between them. Arrows are added between the pictures to show the narrative direction of the story.

A 'Story Map' is often drawn by the teacher on a flipchart that the whole class can see. It acts as a prompt for pupils when they are verbally recounting the story together (often with accompanying gestures and mime). The class may be asked to recount the story several times in unison, before going on to write the story. This form of 'Active Storytelling' is used during 'Talk for Writing' lessons, an embodied and systematic approach to writing which has been popularised and developed by Pie Corbett (with Julia Strong, 2011).

How to set it up

The teacher needs a flipchart and felt pens, or maybe an interactive whiteboard. The title of the story and a list of the characters can be written onto the flipchart first, then the teacher (with the help of the class) recalls (or creates) the story and simultaneously draws a simple series of corresponding pictures that depict the main episodes and actions in the story. The teacher gathers some appropriate words and phrases from the class at each stage of the story and writes them alongside the appropriate picture.

Once the 'Story Map' is complete, the teacher and class recount in unison the story together in a physically animated and expressive way, with continuous reference to the map (see 'Active Storytelling', Section 5.9). This storytelling in unison can be accompanied by repeated gestures that are linked with certain words and/or phrases throughout the storytelling. The teacher will be repeatedly modelling actions and associated gestures throughout and the class will vocally and physically, imitate and mimic their 'Teacher as Storyteller' (Section 5.8). The teacher also needs to point towards the 'Story Map', at appropriate moments, as the story progresses. The teacher and class might actively repeat the story together several times. The 'Story Map' remains visible throughout to remind the class of the narrative sequence and the word and phrases that are being included.

For several years, Pie Corbett and Patrice Baldwin delivered termly 'Talk and Drama for Writing' conferences together across England and Wales. Words and phrases were generated using drama strategies, then gathered as a resource bank for use during the 'Talk for Writing' session.

Some possible 'follow-on' strategies and next steps

- The pictures on the 'Story Map' can be formed as 'Still Images' (Section 5.12) and then brought to life through 'Improvisation' (Section 5.1), which will generate speech for inclusion in the story.

- A character on the 'Story Map' can be questioned for a while, maybe by 'Hot-seating' (Section 5.17) or the 'Teacher-in-Role' (Section 5.2).
- The picture on a 'Story Map' will be a very simple drawing. However, it can be physically recreated and then gradually added to and elaborated upon (see 'Still Images', Section 5.12).
- The simple drawings on the 'Story Map' will each depict an episode in the story. Each drawing can become the stimulus for a short, devised scene (see 'Small Group Playmaking', Section 5.15). The scenes can then be performed sequentially using a 'Performance Carousel' (Section 5.16).

5.41 3D Landscapes

What it offers

There are times when a teacher wants their pupils to give particular attention to a setting. In drama, pupils sometimes position their bodies to collectively represent a landscape setting. They might be physically creating an original landscape or recreating a '3D landscape' from a specific painting or photograph, or one described within a text. They might become an additional feature on a given '3D landscape'. They need to study the image or text carefully first, before making their selection. Once they have entered a landscape and physically become part of it, the landscape will become more memorable.

How to set it up

The class either stand in a large circle, or as three sides of a rectangle. In turn, each pupil enters and positions themselves in the space 'as if' they are a landscape feature. As each pupil gets into position, they clearly state (to an imaginary audience) which landscape feature they are and give some additional information, such as the following.

- 'I am a cliff made of sand. Sand martins nest inside me every spring' (Geography and Science).
- 'I am a mountain. There are different countries on either side of me. I have seen wars' (Geography and History).

Some possible 'follow-on' strategies and next steps

- Once the last pupil is in position, tell the class that you will move around the landscape. Whichever landscape feature you are near, that pupil in role will repeat whatever they previously said as the landscape feature (see 'Eavesdropping', Section 5.5).
- You can walk around the whole landscape, in role as a character (see 'Teacher-in-Role', Section 5.2). As you pass each landscape feature in turn, the pupil in role will talk either to you or about you, e.g. the trees and reeds talking, to or about the Lady of Shalott as she floats towards Camelot (English).

5.42 Talking Objects

What it offers

Pupils can talk in role 'as if' they are objects. They can talk to themselves or talk to other objects or to characters. Objects often belong to characters and might be able to tell us about their owners. Objects may have overheard conversations and witnessed situations and events that they can recount. They may also have been on journeys. Every object will have its own history, and some may have had several owners. Objects can be new or old, and some will have changed in some way, e.g. a teapot might have been dropped and has become chipped. Some objects are hardly noticeable, whereas others are prominent. Objects might become significant, e.g. the dagger with which Macbeth murdered Duncan. Some objects are symbolic and others become symbolic. Some objects in stories have magical powers! Objects can be mass-produced or handmade, commonplace or rare or unique. When pupils talk in role 'as if' they are an object, it can be a helpful step before writing in role as that object (personification). When pupils are studying pictures, paintings, photographs, or film clips (for example) to choose an object to become (in role), they will be noticing various objects within the image. Once they have talked in role as a particular object, that object becomes more memorable.

How to set it up

There are different ways of setting up 'Talking Objects'. The class can be shown a picture that has various objects within it. Every pupil can choose a different object from the picture. The picture is then recreated physically, with each pupil entering the space in turn and positioning themselves 'as if' they are their chosen object. As each object gets into position, it briefly says what it is and adds a little information, e.g. 'I am the paper bird on the mantelpiece. He made me for his daughter' (see Shaun Tan's (2006) graphic novel *The Arrival*).

Linked activities and variations

- Ask the class to sit in a circle. Show them an object and explain that you want them to pass it around the circle. Whoever is holding the object needs to speak in role 'as if' they are that object. They will then pass the object on to the next pupil. On receiving the object, pupils should try to seamlessly continue the object's monologue. Pupils who do not want to take their turn stay in the circle but may silently pass on the object.
- Pupils can be invited to bring in an object they own. The pupil's object is passed around the circle and whoever is holding the object can ask it a question. The owner of the object can answer the question 'as if' they are the object that they brought in.
- Images of historical artefacts and information about them is available on the internet, e.g. objects found in the tomb of Tutankhamun or objects that survived the Great Fire of London. Pupils can each search for an object, find an image of it, and gather information about it for a short presentation to the class. The image of the object can be projected and pupils can each be given the option of either presenting the object out of role, or giving information about it in role, 'as if' the pupil *is* the object talking about itself.

Some possible 'follow on' strategies and next steps

- Some of the class can be in role as 'Talking Objects' and the rest can ask a few questions to each object, (see 'Hot-seating', Section 5.17). Questions should be addressed directly to named, individual objects, e.g. 'Door, does anyone ever come through you and visit the Lady of Shalott?' Objects can avoid answering questions (especially if they don't know the answer), but should try to answer 'in role', e.g. 'I am sorry. I am not going to answer that question'.
- If pupils have positioned themselves as objects within a setting, a character can then pass by each object in turn. The objects can each speak *to* or *about* the character as the character passes by. For example, the objects in the Mead Hall of Heorot can each speak to (or about) Beowulf (the 'teacher in role' (Section 5.2)) as he passes by each of them, whilst waiting for monstrous Grendel to arrive (Baldwin and Galaska, 2022).

Bibliography

Alexander, R.J. (2008) *Towards Dialogic Teaching: Rethinking Classroom Talk*, 4th edition, New York, UK: Dialogoc.
Alexander, R.J. (2017) *The Arts in Schools: Making the Case, Heeding the Evidence*, At the Intercultural Dimensions of Cultural Education Conference, University of Chester.
Baldwin, P. (2004, 2012) *With Drama in Mind – Real Learning in Imagined Worlds*, 1st and 2nd editions, London and New York: Continuum.
Baldwin, P. (2008) *The Primary Drama Handbook*, London, California, New Delhi, Singapore: Sage Publications Ltd.
Baldwin, P. (2019) *The Pied Piper of Hamelin: One-off Workshop*, Drama & Theatre, London: MA Education Ltd.
Baldwin, P. & Fleming, K. (2003) *Teaching Literacy Through Drama – Creative Approaches*, Abingdon and Oxon: Routledge Falmer.
Baldwin, P. & Galaska, A. (2022) *Process Drama for Second Language Teaching and Learning: A Toolkit for Developing Language and Life Skills*, London, New York, Dublin: Bloomsbury Academic.
Baldwin, P. & Hendy, L. (1994). *The Drama Book: An Active Approach to Learning*, London: Collins Educational.
Baldwin, P. & John, R. (2012) *Inspiring Writing through Drama, Creative Approaches to Teaching ages 7 to 16*, London, Delhi, New York, Delhi, Sydney: Bloomsbury.
Barnes, D. (1976) *From Communication to Curriculum*, Harmondsworth: Penguin Education.
Barrie, J.M. (2021) *Peter Pan*, New York: Harper Collins Publishers.
Beck, I. (1995) *Tom and the Island of Dinosaurs*, London: Random House Children's Books.
Boal, A. (1992) *Games for Actors and Non-Actors*, 2nd edition, London: Routledge.
Boal, A. (1995) *The Rainbow of Desire: The Boal Method of Theatre and Therapy*, Oxon: Routledge.
Boal, A. (2019) *Theater of the Oppressed*, 4th edition, London: Pluto Press.
Booth, D. (2005) *Storydrama*, 2nd Revised edition, Toronto, Ontario, Canada: Pembroke Publishing Ltd.
Browning, R. *The Pied Piper of Hamelin*, Poetry Foundation website www.poetryfoundation.org/poems/45818/the-pied-piper-of-hamelin
Cecil, L. (1997) *Noah and the Space Ark*, London: Hamish Hamilton.
Corbett, P. & Strong, J. (2011) *Talk for Writing Across the Curriculum- How to Teach Non-fiction Writing 5-12 Years*, Maidenhead, UK: McGraw-Hill Education.
Greder, A. (2002) *The Island*, NSW, Crows Nest, Australia: Allen & Unwin.
Harrison, M. & Stuart-Clarke, C. (2006) *The Oxford Book of Story Poems*, Oxford and New York: Oxford University Press.
Heathcote, D. & Bolton, G. (1995) *Drama for Learning: Dorothy Heathcote's Mantle of the Expert Approach to Education*, Portsmouth, NH: Heinemann Press.
Hedderwick, M. (1985) *Katie Morag and the Two Grandmothers*, London: Bodley Head.
Johnstone, K. (1987) *Impro: Improvisation and Theatre*, New York: Routledge.
Lewis, C.S. (1970) *The Lion, the Witch and the Wardrobe*, Harmondsworth, Middlesex: Puffin Books.
Littleton, K. & Mercer, N. (2007) *Dialogue and the Development of Children's Thinking: A Socio-Cultural Approach*, London, UK: Routledge.
Littleton, K. & Mercer, N. (2013) *Interthinking: Putting Talk to Work*, London and New York: Routledge.

McCubbin, F. (1904) *The Pioneer*. National Gallery of Victoria, Australia website www.ngv.vic.gov.au/frederick-mccubbin-the-pioneer-1904/
Mercer, N. (2000) *Words and Minds: How We Use Language to Think Together*, London: Routledge.
Mercer, N. (2008) *Three Kinds of Talk*, Cambridge: University of Cambridge, Thinking Together.
Moreno, J.L. (1946) *Psychodrama*, 2nd Revised edition, Ambler, PA: Beacon House.
Moreno: *Understanding People*. website http://moreno.com.au/spectrogram-psychodrama
Mosley, J. (1996) *Quality Circle Time in the Primary Classroom*, Wisbech: LDA.
Mosley, J. & Tew, M. (1999) *Quality Circle Time in the Secondary School – A Handbook of Good Practice*, London: David Fulton Publishers.
Neelands, J. & Goode, T. (1990) *Structuring Drama Work*, Cambridge: Cambridge University Press.
Noyes, A. (1906) *The Highwayman*, Blackwood's Magazine, Edinburgh, UK: William Blackwood and Sons.
Owen, R. *Dulce et Decorum Est*, Poetry Foundation website www.poetryfoundation.org/poems/46560/dulce-et-decorum-est
Resnick, L.B. Asterhan, C.S.C. & Clarke, S.N. (2018) *Accountable Talk: Instructional Dialogue That Builds the Mind*. The International Academy of Education (IAE) and the International Bureau of Education (IBE) of the United Nations Educational, Scientific and Cultural Organization, (UNESCO).
Revans, R. (1998) *ABC of Action Learning*, London: Lemos & Crane.
Schechner, R. (2006) *Performance Studies: An Introduction*, New York: Routledge.
Shaw, A. *The Discovery of King Tut's Tomb*, National Geographic website https://kids.nationalgeographic.com/history/article/the-discovery-of-king-tuts-tomb
Tan, S. (2006) *The Arrival*, Melbourne, Australia: Lothian Books.
Taylor, T. (2016) *Mantle of the Expert- A Transformative Approach to Education*, Norwich: Singular Publishing.
Teachers' TV *Drama for Learning: PSHE Through Drama at Key Stage 2*, website www.youtube.com/watch?v=_uJh94egeWo
Tennyson, A. (1842) *Poems*, Boston: W.D. Ticknor.
Turnbull, A. (1995) *The Last Wolf*, London: Hamish Hamilton.
Varela, F.J., Thompson, E. & Rosch, E. (1991) *The Embodied Mind: Cognitive Science and Human Experience*, Cambridge, MA: MIT Press.
Voice 21 website https://voice21.org/
Wagner, B.J. (1979) *Dorothy Heathcote: Drama as a Learning Medium*. London: Hutchinson.

Art References

Bayeux Tapestry. ca. 1070. Tapestry. Musèe de la Tapisserie de Bayeux, Bayeux, France.
The Great Fire of London. ca. 1675. Painting by Josepha Jane Battlehooke, Museum of London, England.
The Death of Nelson. ca. 1859-64. Painting by Daniel Maclise, National Museums Liverpool, England.
The Pioneer. 1904. Paintings by Frederick McCubbin, National Gallery of Victoria, Melbourne, Australia.
Three Studies for Figures at the Base of a Crucifixion. 1944. Paintings by Francis Bacon. Tate Gallery, London, UK.

Index

Note: Page numbers in *italics* indicate figures or tables on the corresponding pages. Numbers in **bold** indicate the main pages for each strategy.

'3D Landscapes' **100**; of art and design images 31
'3D Storyboard' **63-64**; and PSHE and Relationships Education 63; for writing 24

accountable talk 18
'Active Storytelling' 13, **53-54**; and 'Drama Maps' 97; and 'Story Maps' 98; and 'talking like a writer' 24
ADHD *see* attention deficit hyperactivity disorder
Alexander, Robin 14
attention deficit hyperactivity disorder 57

Baldwin, Patrice 98
Boal's Forum Theatre 19

'Choral Speaking' **86-87**
'Circle Time' 4, 22; and 'passing' 12
class circle 4-9; concentric 7-8, *8*; and pairs 5, *5*; and passing 'it' on 7, *7*; and smaller groups 9, *9*; while 'blind' 5-6, *6*
class lines 9-11; as continuous 10, *10*; with only one moving line 10-11, *11*; and standpoints 9, *9*; and tunnels and corridors 10, *10*
'Collective Role' 12, **85**; and cumulative talk 17; and persuasive speech 17; and thought/speech bubbles 26
communication 4; verbal and non-verbal 12-13
community 4
concentric circle 7-8; and changing partners 7-8, *8*; and talkers and listeners 8, *8*
connection 4

'Conscience Alley' 10, 12, **73**; and disputational talk 19; and listening 21; and the pace of talk 22; and performance of writing frames 25-26; and persuasive speech 17; as a thought and talk frame 14; and 'Thought Collage' 89; *see also* 'Decision Alley'
constraint 11-12
Corbett, Pie 13, 98
'Corridor of Voices' 10, **76**; and cumulative talk 17; and debate 20; and informative speech 20; as a thought and talk frame 14-15; *see also* 'Thought Tunnel'
cumulative talk 17

debate 20
'Decision Alley' 10, **74**; and cumulative talk 17; and debate 20; and performance of writing frames 25-26; and persuasive speech 17; *see also* 'Conscience Alley'
deep learning 3
descriptive talk 16-17
dialogue 15, 28
disputational talk 19
drama contracts 12
'Drama Maps' **96-97**
drama strategies: as continuously evolving 14; and following of protocols 21, 67; and freedom or constraint 11-12; and inclusion 12; to set up a writing task 23-28; types of configurations for 3-11

'Eavesdropping' 12, **46**; and listening 21; and 'Telephone Conversations' 95; as a thought and talk frame 14

embodied cognition 13
explanation 19, 21, 80
exploratory talk 17-18
eye contact 4
'Eyewitness' **47**

focal point 4, 6
freedom 11-12
'Freeze-frame' 3, 11, 13, **56-57**; in '3D Storyboard' 63; in 'Eavesdropping' 46; in 'Performance Carousel' 67
'Freeze if. . .' **82**

gesture *see* movement
group circles 9, *9*

Heathcote, Dorothy 44-45, 97
'Hot-seating' 3, 12, **69-70**; and questioning 15-16; and 'Story Map' 99

images 29; of art and design 31-32, 58; construction and deconstruction of 32, 58-59; contrasting of 32-33, 60-61; of English literature 29-30, 58; entering and elaborating on 30, 32, 38, 58, 60; of geography 30; historic 29, 58; and PSHE and Relationships Education 30-31, 58-59; visualising of 33
'Improvisation' 11, **37-39**; in '3D Storyboard' 63; of art and design images 31; and historic images 29; and maps 28; and 'Story Map' 98; in 'Voice Collage' 88
inanimate objects: as animated 26-27, 101
inclusion 4; during drama strategies 12
informative speech 20
'in role' 3, 16, 95; as an object 101; and disputes 19
instruments 90, 93
internal monologue 15, 77
interthinking 14

justification 19, 21, 80

listening 21; to avoid repetition 21
Littleton, K. 14

'Mantle of the Expert' **44-45**, *45*; and accountable talk 18; and presentational talk in role 20; and writing tasks 25
maps 27-28, 30, 96-97, 98-99

'Meetings' **42-43**; and dialogue 15
Mercer, N. 14
miming 11, 12-13; to recount a story 53-54, 55; *see also* movement
Moreno, Jacob 4
'Move if. . .' **81**
movement 12-13; in slow motion 13

'overheard conversations' *see* 'Eavesdropping'

passing 12, 55
'Passing Thoughts' 4, *4*, 12, **78**; and accountable talk 18; and cumulative talk 17; and equal opportunities to talk 21-22; and the pace of talk 22; in 'Rumours' 50; as a thought and talk frame 14, 15; and thought bubbles 26
performance 3; of writing frames 25-26
'Performance Carousel' 9, 13, 24, **67-68**; in 'Small Group Playmaking' 65; and 'Sound Collage' 91; and 'Story Map' 99
'performance dust' 46
persuasive speech 17
polyptych 63
presentational talk 20; 'in role' 20
'Proxemics' 7, **79**; and accountable talk 18; and disputational talk 19
psychodrama 4; and concentric circles 8

questioning 15-16, 69-70, 102

reasoning 19
reflection 19
responsibility 4
'Role on the Wall' *83*, **83-84**; and character studies 25; and 'Hot-seating' 70; and informative speech 20; and 'Passing Thoughts' 78; and 'Proxemics' 79; in 'Rumours' 50; and 'Thought-tracking' 72
'Rumours' 11-12, **49-50**; and improvised dialogue 15; and listening 21; as a thought and talk frame 14

Schechner, Richard 3
'Sculpting' **62**; of art and design images 31; and construction and deconstruction of an image 32
'Sensory Journey' **94**; and imaginary settings 27

sentence stems 18-19; to describe imagery 30; during descriptive talk 16-17; examples of 19; and informative speech 20

settings: as animated 27; for 'Improvisation' 37-8; making sense of imaginary 27, 94; mapping of 27-28

Shakespeare, William 11, 30

'Small Group Playmaking' **65-66**; of art and design images 31; and dialogue 15; and historic images 29; and maps 28; and sequencing scenes 65; and 'split screen' scenes 65; and 'Teacher as Storyteller' 51-2

sociodrama 4

sound 90-93

'Sound Collage' 12, **90-91**; and listening 21

'Soundscape' **92**

'Sound Story' **93**

spatial positioning 79

speaking object 7, 7, 22

'Spectrogram' see 'Spectrum of Difference'

'Spectrum of Difference' **80**; and accountable talk 18; and disputational talk 19; in 'Rumours' 50

staging columns 11, *11*

status 4

'Still Images and Tableaus' 13, 24, **58-61**; of art and design images 31, 58; and construction and deconstruction of an image 32, 58-59; and 'Freeze-frame' 56; and historic images 29, 58; and illustration of a written story 28; and images of literature 29-30, 58; and PSHE and Relationships Education 30-31, 58-59; and 'Story Map' 98

stillness 13

storyboard 24, 63

story-drama 23-24

'Story Maps' 27-28, **98-99**

storytelling 23-24, 51

'Talk for Writing' approach 13, 98

'Talking Objects' **101-102**

'Talking Partners' 5, *5*

teacher: and adapting strategies for their purposes 15; as participant in drama strategies 12, 16, 40-41; and their choice of role in student writing tasks 25

'Teacher as Storyteller' **51-52**; and 'Story Maps' 98; and 'talking like a writer' 24

'Teacher-in-Role' 12, **40-41**; and dialogue 15; in 'Eyewitness' 48; in 'Hot-seating' 69; and information giving 20; in 'Mantle of the Expert' 44; in 'Meetings' 42-43; in 'Rumours' 49; and 'Story Map' 99; and writing tasks 25

'Telephone Conversations' **95**; and improvised dialogue 15

theatre in the round 6, *6*, 52

'thought and talk' frames 14; and equal opportunities to speak 21-22; and varying the pace of talk 22

'Thought Collage' **89**; and listening 21; and the pace of talk 22; as a thought and talk frame 14; and 'Thought-tracking 72

'Thought-tracking' **71-72**; and disputational talk 19; as a thought and talk frame 14, 15; and thought bubbles 26, 71-72; and 'Thought Collage' 89

'Thought Tunnel' 10, **75**; as a thought and talk frame 14; and thought bubbles 26; *see also* 'Corridor of Voices'

'Thought-walk' **77**; as a thought and talk frame 14, 15; and thought bubbles 26; and verbal flow of content 26

triptych 31-32, 63

voice 12-13, 86-88

'Voice Collage' 12, **88**; and 'Decision Alley' 74; and listening 21; and the pace of talk 22; in 'Rumours' 50; as a thought and talk frame 14

'Whoosh!' 4, 5, 12, 13, **55**; and 'talking like a writer' 24

writing 23; and '3D Storyboarding' 24; about fictional settings 27-28; about inanimate objects 26-27; and character studies 25; and 'Eyewitness' 47; frames 25-26; and illustration through short scenes 28; in role during a story-drama 23-24, 28; and role of the teacher 25; and 'Role on the Wall' 83; of thought and speech bubbles 26; and verbally recounting a narrative 28; and the 'walk and talk' 26

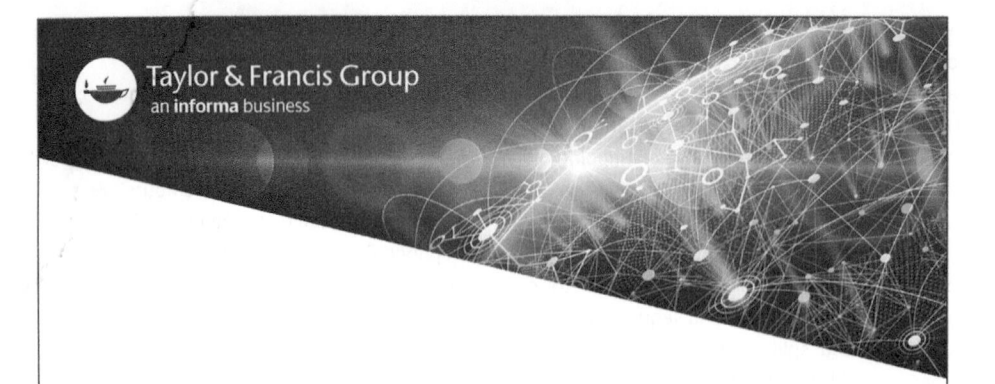

Taylor & Francis eBooks

www.taylorfrancis.com

A single destination for eBooks from Taylor & Francis with increased functionality and an improved user experience to meet the needs of our customers.

90,000+ eBooks of award-winning academic content in Humanities, Social Science, Science, Technology, Engineering, and Medical written by a global network of editors and authors.

TAYLOR & FRANCIS EBOOKS OFFERS:

- A streamlined experience for our library customers
- A single point of discovery for all of our eBook content
- Improved search and discovery of content at both book and chapter level

REQUEST A FREE TRIAL
support@taylorfrancis.com